PENGUIN BOOKS

For all the You Choose readers who spent the last eight years asking for more. Thank you so much for your enthusiasm and patience.

PENGUIN BOOKS

UK | USA | Canada | Ireland | Australia
India | New Zealand | South Africa | China

Penguin Random House Australia is part of the Penguin Random House group of companies whose addresses can be found at global.penguinrandomhouse.com.

First published by Penguin, an imprint of Penguin Random House Australia Pty Ltd, in 2025

Cover and internal illustrations by James Hart
Cover design by Christa Moffitt, Christabella Designs
Internal design and typesetting by Midland Typesetters, Australia
Printed and bound in Australia by Griffin Press, an accredited
ISO AS/NZS 14001 Environmental Management Systems printer

A catalogue record for this book is available from the National Library of Australia

ISBN 978 1 76135 349 9 (Paperback)

We at Penguin Random House Australia acknowledge that Aboriginal and Torres Strait Islander peoples are the Traditional Custodians and the first storytellers of the lands on which we live and work. We honour Aboriginal and Torres Strait Islander peoples' continuous connection to Country, waters, skies and communities. We celebrate Aboriginal and Torres Strait Islander stories, traditions and living cultures; and we pay our respects to Elders past and present.

ROAAAAAR!

The terrifying sound echoes all around you, freezing you in place. You hear branches splintering and feel the ground shake with heavy footfalls. A massive reptilian head rears up over the treetops. OMG . . . it's a Tyrannosaurus rex. Your legs feel like jelly and your heart is pounding overtime. Not even your love of dinosaurs could have prepared you for this moment.

The creature's jaws open wide as it bellows again, and you see the rows of sharp blade-like teeth designed to slash the flesh of its prey. No, this is not a T-rex after all. This dinosaur has much sharper teeth than good old T. It must be a Giganotosaurus. It's about thirty million years older and, head to tail, a little bit longer than the more famous apex predator. You're pretty pleased with yourself for figuring that out.

But knowing the difference between these carnivorous killing-machines is not going to do you much good in this situation. So . . .

What *are* you going to do?

Your first instinct is to run away.
To do so, go to page 16.

But it's such a fascinating creature.
And seeing it up close like this is so cool!
Maybe you should stay where you are and face it?
Go to page 4.

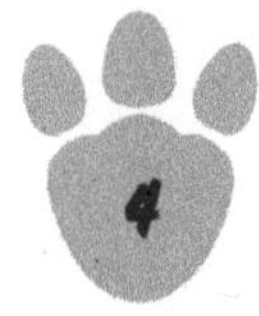

You decide to stay and face the Gigano-tosaurus. After all, you are here for ADVENTURE and what could be more adventurous than this? But perhaps a little help would be a good idea?

You rummage through your backpack to see what you've got in your inventory.

You pull out a taser. Hmmm? You're not sure it would do much good on such a HUMONGOUS dinosaur. You reach back in. There's only one other item – a small packet of Dino Snacks. 'The irresistible snack that no dinosaur could possibly resist.' You cringe at the dodgy marketing slogan and wince at how tiny the packet is. Could such a small snack satisfy the hunger of such a big beast?

Which will you use?

To use the taser, go to page 5.

To use the Dino Snacks, go to page 14.

You decide to go with the taser.

Taking a deep breath, you run at the Giganotosaurus. You jump up onto its foot and jam the taser into the thick scaly hide of its leg, repeatedly zapping it. It does not render the beast unconscious, as you had vainly hoped. It doesn't even disorientate it. All it seems to have done is made it mad.

The creature leans down, flailing at you with its useless little arms. It may not be a T-rex, but this dinosaur's arms are just as small. You're about to laugh at it, when it lifts its leg off the ground. You lose your balance and fall, landing hard on your backside. You're not laughing now.

You look up to see the foot coming back down towards you. You don't even have time to scream as it squashes you flat.

In a burst of pixelating static, you are expelled from the immersive game. You take off your helmet and climb out of the virtual reality pod. Another student eagerly takes your place.

There is a row of ten egg-shaped VR pods in the Welcome Lounge of the Dynamic Dinosaur Discovery Complex. You see your friends are still in their pods. They seemed to have survived longer than you. But at least you've had a turn. There are other students still waiting to have a go.

'Okay, students! It's time to start the excursion.' Your teacher, Mr Hendrickson, walks along the length of the pods. 'Please exit the games and come along. Now!' His voice is quite insistent.

Some of your classmates begin climbing out of the pods. Others are looking annoyed at having missed out on a game.

'Don't worry,' calls Mr Hendrickson. 'You'll get another chance to have a go at the virtual reality. Now, all of you, come over here.'

Your teacher, clipboard in hand, moves to the far side of the Lounge, the other students following him. You rush over to join them, wondering what will be next.

Go to page 8.

'Okay class,' says Mr Hendrickson, 'gather round.'

You and your classmates crowd together beside your teacher.

'I hope I don't need to remind you all to be on your best behaviour.' Oh no, he's gone into lecture mode. 'We are amongst the first schools to be visiting the Dynamic Dinosaur Discovery Complex. It has not even opened to the public yet. This is quite a privilege and an extraordinary opportunity. So do not waste it! Make the most of this experience.' He glares pointedly at you as he says this.

You smile back, giving him your best *you-can-trust-me* expression, while crossing your fingers behind your back.

'Assuming you all did your homework reading, you know that this island complex is divided into three areas. The main outdoor exhibition area is the Animatronics Park with life-sized replica dinosaurs. This is where most visitors will be going once the Complex opens properly. And this is where you'll get to spend most of today. You should all have question sheets that you will need to fill out as you look around.'

Of course you did your homework reading. In fact, you even did extra reading on the ferry journey to the island this morning.

'Then there's the Research and Education Centre. The palaeontology exhibition within has been specifically designed for schools. You will get to go through there in smaller groups. And finally there are a number of research areas. These spaces are not open to the public. They are clearly marked, so please stay out of these areas. Except . . .' He pauses for dramatic effect. '. . . you will get to go on a special guided tour of the DNA research facilities. Exciting stuff!'

He takes a deep breath before continuing. How long is this briefing going to take? You are eager for the dinosaurs.

'Okay, so I'm going to send a group of you on the first of the tours now. Then I'll sort the rest of you into two more groups and give you your times. Who would like to be in the first group?'

Do you want to go to the Research and Education Centre for the first tour?
Go to page 88.

Or would you rather start outside with the Animatronics Park?
Go to page 20.

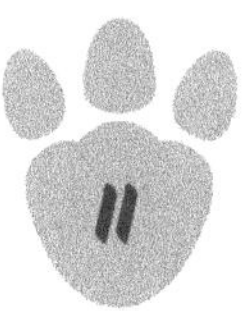

You decide it's best to explore on your own. You fish out your school question sheet and wander about, checking out the dinosaur exhibits and the information signs beside each. Answering the questions is fairly easy. In fact, you could answer most of these off the top of your head.

The word dinosaur comes from the Greek words deinos *and* sauros. *What does the name mean?* Simple! Terrible lizard.

Is the Stegosaurus a herbivore, carnivore or omnivore? Too easy! Herbivore.

The remains of plants and animals preserved in rock are called what? Fossils.

Which dinosaur had the strongest bite? Your fave . . . the Tyrannosaurus rex!

You knock off the questions real quick and then go check out the Gasparinisaura. It's a small herbivorous ornithopod, about knee height and kind of cute. It's a mottled greeny-brown colour

but has red stripy patches along its spine. The animatronic is quite lifelike; its head darts from side to side, before it bends down to munch on a small shrub.

You're about to continue on when you spot movement in the undergrowth behind it. You go right up to the rope barrier and peer into the vegetation. A pair of eyes are staring back at you. It's another Gasparinisaura. You wonder why they'd hide an animatronic in amongst the bushes like that, where people can't see it properly. It seems a bit odd.

You hear shouting from behind and turn around. A security guard is yelling at your friends Jake and Jen. The two of them are standing next to a Triceratops. They must have stepped over the rope barrier to get a closer look . . . and now they're being told off.

The sound of rustling branches makes you turn back to the half-hidden Gasparinisaura. It turns around and hops off into the trees.

WHAT?

That couldn't have happened! Surely an animatronic couldn't run off like that. You must have imagined it!

You're about to go into the trees to check, when more shouting makes you turn around again. Your friends are running and the security guard is chasing them.

To chase after your friends, go to page 46.

To follow the Gasparinisaura, go to page 22.

You go for the Dino Snacks.

You frantically try to open the packet, but the seal won't give. You desperately tear at it with your teeth. Still no luck!

ROAAAAAR!

You look up to see the Giganotosaurus leaning down towards you. You gag as you feel its hot, stinky breath. You can see into its ravenous mouth, saliva dripping down onto you. In desperation, you throw the unopened Dino Snacks packet directly into its gaping maw.

The beast gulps it down and pauses. Then it backs away, turns and goes crashing off into the forest.

You breathe a sigh of relief. Who knew that marketing could work so well?

You are about to continue your explorations, when you hear a distant voice calling.

'Okay, students! It's time to start the excursion.'

But there's still so much to explore in this immersive virtual reality game.

'Please exit the games and come along. Now!' The teacher's voice is quite insistent.

To comply with your teacher and exit the game, go to page 19.

To ignore your teacher and continue playing, go to page 24.

Without hesitation, you bolt!

Branches smack you in the face and thorns tear at your clothes as you race through the jungle. You can feel the ground tremble and hear the trees being flattened with each pursuing Giganotosaurus footstep.

You put on an extra burst of speed! Your heart is beating even faster now, the blood rushing in your ears.

You run and run and run until you feel like you can run no more. But still you push on.

Until you realise you can no longer hear the dinosaur. Has it given up? Are you safe?

You allow yourself to slow down. But as you do, the ground beneath you disappears and you're tumbling through the undergrowth, down into a ditch.

With a thud, you come to a sudden stop. You look around. You're in a nest, surrounded by eggs – eggs about the size of mangos. For a

moment you're really hungry, visions of sizzling bacon and eggs rising up in your imagination. But then you notice one of the eggs is cracking.

You watch as a little reptilian claw breaks through the shell. Then the egg beside it also begins to crack. Seconds later, all the other eggs are fracturing and breaking, the baby dinosaurs making their way out.

You gaze at them in awe. You're pretty sure they're some sort of raptor. You wonder if they'll mistake you for their mother. But then they're all staring at you with hunger in their eyes. The closest one to you opens its mouth, showing you its needle-like teeth. They all begin to wobble towards you, making little growling sounds as their mouths snap open and closed. You try to back away, but they are all around you.

You are wondering what you're going to do, when you hear a distant voice calling.

'Okay, students! It's time to start the excursion.'

That's good timing on the part of your teacher.

‘Please exit the games and come along. Now!’ The teacher’s voice is quite insistent.

As the first baby raptor launches itself at your face . . .

You exit the game.

Go to page 19.

You take off your helmet and climb out of the VR pod.

There is a row of ten egg-shaped VR pods in the Welcome Lounge of the Dynamic Dinosaur Discovery Complex. You see some of your classmates climbing out of them. Others are looking annoyed at having missed out on a game.

'Don't worry,' calls Mr Hendrickson. 'You'll get another chance to have a go at the virtual reality. Now, all of you, come over here.'

Your teacher, clipboard in hand, moves to the far side of the Lounge, the other students following him. You rush over to join them, wondering what will be next.

Go to page 8.

You decide to start with the replica dinosaurs. Mr Hendrickson assigns you to Group 2. You have an hour and a half to explore the Animatronics Park before needing to meet up in the Research and Education Centre for the tour. You head outside.

The area is set up a bit like a zoo. There are paths winding their way through forested areas, with roped-off sections containing dinosaurs. The dinosaurs look amazingly real! The only thing that gives them away as animatronics is their limited range of movements.

There are kids from various schools wandering around looking at the exhibits. There are also some teachers. You are a bit surprised at how many security guards are patrolling the grounds.

'Are you coming?'

You see your two best friends, Jake and Jen, heading towards one of the dinosaurs. Even though they're your friends, you know they have

a knack for getting into trouble – especially Jen. Given the way Mr Hendrickson looked at you earlier, you wonder if it's a good idea to go with them.

To go with your friends,
go to page 27.

To explore on your own,
go to page 11.

Jake and Jen have got themselves into trouble. It's their problem, not yours. And the glimpse of the creature in the undergrowth is just too intriguing to pass up.

You jump the rope barrier, race past the animatronic Gasparinisaura, and go into the forested area. You can see and hear movement up ahead. You make your way in that direction and are led to a little clearing.

There, the creature you have been following comes to a stop. It's definitely a Gasparinisaura. You gaze at it in astonishment. It's not an animatronic. But is it real? That would be impossible!

You notice it has a plastic tube secured by a band around its neck. You wonder what that could be.

The dinosaur cocks its head to one side, then dashes off. You follow. It's fast, but you manage to keep up as it leads you down paths marked 'Staff Only'.

Finally, it reaches a super-high fence. There is a huge sign by the gate: 'ANIMATRONICS & ROBOTICS – RESTRICTED AREA'. Robotics? Maybe that little dinosaur that you've been following is actually a sophisticated robot.

As the Gasparinisaura approaches, there is an electronic buzz and the gate opens. The dinosaur enters, then stops as if to see if you'll follow. Do you?

To enter, go to page 34.

To return to the Animatronics Park, go to page 53.

You decide to ignore your teacher. After all, it's something you have a lot of experience with. And you never get into any real trouble. You can always claim you didn't hear him.

You head off into the jungle, in the opposite direction to the Giganotosaurus.

It's not long before the vegetation thins and you reach the end of the jungle. You peer through the last of the undergrowth to see a scene straight out of *Jurassic Park.*

A herd of Apatosauruses are gathered by a huge lake. They are about the same size as Brachiosaurs, but with stumpier legs and thicker necks. Several of them are at the edge of the water, necks bent down, drinking. A few others are munching on the scraggly bushes. A small group of Lesothosauruses tear at long tufts of grass with their beaks. These waist-high dinosaurs are feathered and somewhat bird-like. A couple of Pterosaurs circle above in the air, gliding on their leathery wings. They are too high for you to be able to discern the species.

You hear your teacher's voice again, but you are so engrossed in the scene before you that you don't take any notice of it.

A sound to your left draws your attention. In amongst the vegetation you see movement. Then, without any further warning, four Allosauruses streak from the cover of the jungle, heading straight for the lake. About twice your height, these scaly green hunters are like sleek, mini T-rexes. The Lesothosauruses scatter. But the Apatosauruses are slower to react. As they turn to lumber off, the Allosauruses strike.

Everything freezes.

What's going on?

You take off your helmet and climb out of the VR pod to be faced by angry eyes, flaring nostrils and a form way scarier than any dinosaur.

It's your teacher, Mr Hendrickson. And he's NOT happy.

Towering over you, he glares with barely contained rage. His voice is controlled but he's talking through clenched teeth.

'I have had enough of you. You have ignored me for the last time.' He holds up a quivering finger to stop you from responding. 'Not only have you held up the other students, all of whom responded when I called, but you have also inconvenienced the staff here. Do you realise what a privilege it is to be here today? We are amongst the first schools to visit the Dynamic Dinosaur Discovery Complex. You were warned to be on your best behaviour . . .'

You are escorted back to the ferry that brought you and your fellow students to the island where the Complex is located. You look around you as you go, taking in all the sights and experiences that you will be missing out on – the Research and Education Centre with its huge dome and dinosaur bone exhibition, and the Animatronics Park full of life-sized moving dinosaurs. Instead, you will be sitting on the ferry, all alone, writing an essay on missed opportunities.

You catch up with your friends, Jake and Jen, as they head towards the T-rex. It is massive. You shiver, remembering the Giganotosaurus you faced in the VR game. The animatronic creature roars then bends down, mouth gaping wide, before straightening up again.

It repeats the sequence of movements, but this time there's a spark and a wisp of smoke from its head as it grinds to a halt – bent over with its mouth open.

A technician wearing a grey uniform runs up to the dinosaur and examines it. You hear her speaking into her walkie-talkie.

'Tech 1 to base. Rex is on the fritz again. Better take 'im offline.'

You and your friends watch as she races off.

'Come on.' Your friends vault the rope barrier and whip out their phones for selfies, waving for you to join them. Hesitantly you jump the rope and pose.

Jen steps back with her phone. 'Stick your head in the T-rex's mouth. It'll make such a cool pic.'

You don't think you should, but Jake is now egging you on. What do you do?

To put your head in the dinosaur's mouth for a photo, go to page 29.

To be sensible and refuse, go to page 30.

What harm could it do? You grab onto the T-rex's teeth as if you're holding its mouth open and tentatively insert your head.

'That's so cool!' calls Jake.

'Yeah,' say Jen and she snaps a few photos. 'Awesome pics!'

You feel the teeth shudder as a spark sizzles somewhere in the beast's mouth. Jake screams! You let go of the teeth and begin to extract your head, but . . .

You're too late.

SNAP!

The jaws clamp shut and your visit to the Dynamic Dinosaur Discovery Complex is over. Permanently!

You know that sticking your head in the animatronic's mouth is just asking for trouble. You refuse.

'Your choice!' Jake shrugs, turning away and taking out his school question sheet.

But Jen doesn't give up and she keeps taunting you. The two of you get into a full-on argument. Suddenly, in frustration, Jen shoves you. 'You are such a wuss!' You trip over the rope barrier and land hard on your rear end.

You know that Jen has a bit of a temper. You know that you should just drop it and move on. But do you?

To stay down and defuse the situation, go to page 32.

But Jen pushed you. It was unprovoked and you are angry. To get up and push her back, go to page 42.

You return to the VR game pods in the Welcome Lounge. But they are all in use. And there's a line of students waiting to have a go.

You notice there's a game pod over in a darkened corner with a sign saying 'Not in use'. It might be worth a try. If it works, then you won't have to wait.

To try out the 'Not in use' pod,
go to page 92.

To demonstrate patience and wait in line,
go to page 91.

You stay down on the ground and look up at Jen. You tell her that if she's going to be picking fights with you, that you no longer want to be her friend.

And suddenly, all the anger drains from her face.

'I'm sorry!' she says, extending a hand and helping you up.

You get to your feet and accept the apology.

Jake comes over and waves the school question sheet at you. 'Now that you're both behaving like human beings again, maybe we should work on this?'

You hear a sizzling, sparking sound from behind you and look around. The faulty animatronic T-rex's jaws snap shut. You gulp and stare at the beast. If you had put your head in its mouth . . .

You shudder at the thought. Jen looks at you with wide eyes. Then breaks into a grin and laughs.

As technicians and guards come running, you and your friends back away.

The three of you spend the next hour and a half wandering around the Park, looking at the awesome exhibits (but staying well behind the rope barriers), reading the information signs and filling out your sheets.

When you're finished, you check the time and realise that you need to get to the Research and Education Centre. You're scheduled to be part of the next group. But your friends are part of the last group.

Jen suggests that you stay with them and go to the Centre later when it's their turn. But Mr Hendrickson had been very clear that you had to go with your assigned group. Do you risk making him angry?

To stay with Jake and Jen,
go to page 36.

To head to the Research and Education Centre
straight away, go to page 88.

Yes, of course you enter!

You walk through an open area that looks a bit like a junkyard. There are bits of discarded animatronics strewn all over the place, as well as piles of scrap metal and rusted electronics.

The Gasparinisaura leads you to a large building that looks like it might be a warehouse.

Entering, you discover it's a massive workshop. You are immediately drawn to the two incomplete T-rexes. The first is just a skeleton, the bones towering over you. It is quite intimidating. The next, however, is a bit repulsive.

This T-rex is all muscles and tendons and ligaments, a few bones visible around the face. It looks like it's been skinned. Why would anyone make an animatronic dinosaur like that?

There are other dinosaurs in various stages of construction around the workshop, but it is the T-rexes that fascinate you. The Gasparinisaura, however, continues on through the workshop.

To continue following the Gasparinisaura,
go to page 38.

To hang back and get a closer look at the T-rexes,
go to page 54.

You decide to take the risk and stay with your friends. The three of you have a marvellous time checking out all the animatronic dinosaurs. There are so many of them! It's easy for you to imagine what it must have been like living in prehistoric times.

At one point you think you see a small creature run through an area of trees and undergrowth behind one of the animatronic displays. Is it a knee-height dinosaur? No . . . impossible! You point it out to your friends, but it's gone by the time they look. It must have been your imagination getting the better of you.

Eventually it's time to head to the Research and Education Centre for Jake and Jen's scheduled tour. Mr Hendrickson is ticking names off a list on his clipboard as you approach. When he sees you coming, his face darkens.

You are in BIG trouble!

You make up a story about getting lost, but he doesn't believe you. He won't let you go on the tour with your friends. Instead, he dumps you in a small waiting room, telling you to write an essay on the existential importance of time management and how it relates to school excursions and future prospects of a successful life.

Writing an essay while everyone else is enjoying themselves is the last thing you want to do. Especially when you don't even understand the topic. Perhaps you could sneak out and have another go at the VR game? But if you get caught you'll end up in even more trouble.

To play it safe, stay put and write the essay, go to page 50.

To go back to the VR game, go to page 31.

You continue to follow the Gasparinisaura. It disappears through a door at the end of the workshop. You're met by a most unexpected scene. There's a strange woman in grease-stained overalls. She has a mop of curly white hair and a huge grin on her face as she holds an ice cream cone out for the dinosaur. The creature is happily licking away at it.

So it's not a robot.

The Gasparinisaura stops licking the ice cream to look at you. The woman follows the creature's line of sight to greet you with a sharp intake of breath. She drops the ice cream, which the dinosaur continues to lick.

'What are you doing here?' she demands. 'This is a restricted area. There are things here you ain't allowed to see or even know about.'

You explain that you followed one of the things you're not supposed to see or know about. She points a finger at the dinosaur and admonishes it.

'Gaspar, you know better than to be followed. Your daddy would be mighty angry if he knew.'

Daddy?

'Mr Richly,' explains the woman. 'The owner of . . . well, everything around here.'

Oh, you've read about him. Mr Titus B Richly, reclusive gazillionaire. He's funded dinosaur research for years. More recently, he bought this entire island and set up the Dynamic Dinosaur Discovery Complex.

'Oh, he's done a lot more than that,' says the woman, indicating Gaspar. 'Cloning, for instance.' She sticks out a hand for you to shake. 'The name's Mavis. Robotics engineer. I look after the animatronics and I'm working on stuff for a new robotic display we're hoping to open up in a year or so.'

You crouch down beside Gaspar and reach out a hand. He allows you to pat him. You ask about the plastic tube.

'Gaspar is one of Mr Richly's messenger dinos,' she explains.

Surely there are better ways of sending messages?

'Yeah, well, Mr Richly's a little . . . eccentric,' says Mavis. 'He likes all his secret communications to be via messenger dino. They have a network of underground tunnels. But Gaspar here prefers to stay above ground. I guess it might be my fault. He likes to visit me on the way to and from his daddy's.'

The dinosaur shivers.

'Poor thing,' adds Mavis. 'Daddy isn't the nicest person, is he?' She then turns her attention to you. 'You can't tell anyone about this. In fact, it'll be safer if you just forget you saw any of this, okay?'

Safer? You nod slowly but know there's no way you'll be able to forget any of this. Nevertheless, you assure Mavis that you'll go straight back to the Animatronics Park. But do you really?

To go back to the Animatronics Park,
go to page 53.

To sneakily continue following Gaspar,
go to page 43.

You know it's a stupid thing to do but you are so angry! You jump to your feet and push Jen back. She stumbles but doesn't fall over. Regaining her balance, she charges at you, ready to fight.

But you've had enough. You don't want to fight her. After all, she's supposed to be your friend. So, as she comes at you, you leap out of the way.

Jen stumbles past you, right into the mouth of the faulty animatronic T-rex. The beast shudders and a spark sizzles at the corner of its mouth.

SNAP!

The jaws clamp shut on Jen.

You run over to the T-rex, yanking at its mouth, trying desperately to get it to release your friend.

But it's all over for her. She won't be picking any more fights with you . . . or anyone else! Ever!

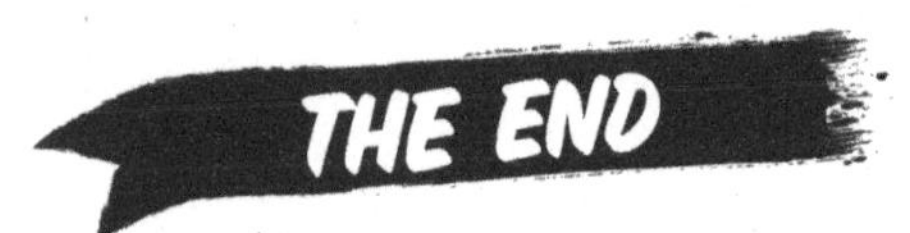

You say goodbye to Mavis but hide behind a pile of scrap outside the workshop until you see Gaspar depart. Then you follow. It's quite a long walk, but you eventually get to Richly's estate – a mansion surrounded by a high wall. There are many signs on the wall:

PRIVATE PROPERTY

KEEP OUT

THIS MEANS YOU

RESTRICTED

NO ENTRY

TRESPASSERS WILL BE EXECUTED

You get the feeling he's not big on visitors. And you hope that last sign is a joke.

Gaspar leads you under the wall through a hidden tunnel. The house and garden are immaculate. The mansion is massive and you can see a glass dome at the far end of it.

Gaspar trots past a display of topiary dinosaurs and approaches a courtyard with a Triceratops

fountain in the centre of a rather large pond. You reckon the marble Triceratops looks like it's projectile puking.

The Gasparinisaura enters the house through a set of French doors. You sneak up to the entrance and peer in.

Richly is seated in a plush armchair beside an open fireplace, surrounded by floor-to-ceiling bookshelves. Gaspar hops up to him. The man stands up with the aid of a walking stick and takes the tube from the dinosaur. He squints through half-moon glasses at the note contained therein. The tycoon is quite old, with swept-back white hair and a neat goatee beard. He's dressed in a safari suit that looks like it came from the 1970s.

'It seems the DNA scientists finally have a new clone for us,' says Richly.

'About blinking time. Given how much I pay them, you'd think they would be more efficient. Anyway, we should go welcome it. Yes?'

A new clone? You wonder what he's referring to. Perhaps you should reveal yourself and ask? But you remember all the signs and think maybe it would be better to stay hidden?

To step inside and say hello,
go to page 55.

To stay hidden, go to page 51.

You can't abandon your friends if they're in trouble . . . even if it is their own fault. You take off after them.

They lead you on a merry chase throughout the Animatronics Park. Other kids stare as you run past. Jake and Jen are laughing and seem to be having a marvellous time, occasionally looking back over their shoulders and taunting the guard. He's a short, podgy, middle-aged guy who's having trouble keeping up.

Your friends race down a path, past signs saying 'Staff Only'. You put on a burst of speed, overtake the guard and catch up with Jake and Jen just as they reach a dead end. In front of you is a high wire-mesh fence with signs saying 'Keep Out' and 'Restricted'. There are thick brambles on either side. You suggest going back the way you came, but the security guard is blocking your escape.

He's slowed down to a walk now and is talking into his walkie-talkie between gasping breaths. 'Request backup . . . restricted area . . . side gate . . . three kids . . .' He puts away the walkie-talkie and grins. 'The three of you are in for it now!'

What? But you haven't done anything wrong. You were just following. You try to explain, but the guard won't listen. He's back on the walkie-talkie again, describing the three of you.

'Over the fence,' Jen suggests.

'On the count of three,' agrees Jake.

But it's a restricted area.

Jen counts down. 'Three . . . two . . . one . . .'

Jake yells, 'NOW!'

Do you go with them?

To jump and climb the fence with your friends, go to page 48.

To stay where you are, go to page 49.

You've come this far. You might as well go all the way. Jake yells 'NOW!' and you jump for the fence with your friends. Soaring through the air, you notice a sign that's fallen: 'CAUTION: HIGH VOLTAGE'.

As your hands connect with the wire, your fingers going through the mesh and gripping tight, pain jolts through your body.

Oh no!

It's an electric fence!

Your body spasms. Sparks erupt around you. A burnt smell fills your nostrils. And your ears are overwhelmed with the sound of your own screaming.

Everything goes black!

'NOOOOO!'

You shout at your friends as you notice a fallen sign: 'CAUTION: HIGH VOLTAGE'. But it's too late.

As their hands connect with the wire fence, you hear the crackle of electricity.

Oh no!

It's an electric fence!

You see their bodies spasm as sparks shower down around them. They're screaming, but they are unable to let go, their fingers caught in the mesh.

Then they go limp, falling to the ground. An awful silence descends. The rest of the day goes by in a blur. You remember ambulances and paramedics. You recall being questioned by teachers and guards and police and reporters and goodness knows who else.

You are traumatised for life!

You decide it's best to play it safe. You remain in the waiting room and write the essay. On the ferry returning to the mainland, you have to endure listening to your friends going on and on and on about how much fun they've had today.

For the next two weeks, you're studying dinosaurs at school. It's a constant reminder of your trip to the Dynamic Dinosaur Discovery Complex and all that you missed out on. But after that unit of study is over, you put the whole thing out of your mind.

So you are taken by surprise at your school's end of year assembly, when you receive first place for your essay in the annual persuasive writing contest. It seems that Mr Hendrickson was so impressed by it that he entered it for you.

And guess what the prize is?

A family pass to the Dynamic Dinosaur Discovery Complex!

You decide to stay hidden and watch. Richly and Gaspar move off further into the house and upstairs. You follow, keeping out of sight, as they make their way to the dome you saw earlier. The two of them climb into some sort of glass enclosure and then they're gone. You come out of hiding and step into the room.

It is breathtaking. The glass walls and dome look out over a forested expanse. In the distance, beyond the trees, you can see buildings and huge cages. A large tube of glass and steel extends from the room, over the trees to those buildings. There's a row of capsules with seats at the entrance to the tube. It's obviously some sort of transportation system.

You look out through the glass to see the capsule with Richly and Gaspar travelling through the tube over the trees. You wonder what's at the other end. Should you enter the next capsule and follow? You are burning with an intense curiosity. But what if you get caught? You have a slightly uneasy feeling about Richly. It might be best to stay away from him.

To follow Richly, go to page 58.

To return to the Animatronics Park and try to forget everything you've seen, go to page 53.

You lose your nerve and go back to the Animatronics Park. You spend the rest of the day doing only the things you are supposed to do. You stay out of trouble, but you find it difficult to enjoy yourself or even pay attention. You keep wondering what you missed out on.

You will never know.

You can't help yourself. You need to get a closer look at that skinned T-rex. Yes, it's kind of disgusting, but it's also kind of fascinating. You gaze at the way the muscles and tendons connect and merge. It is incredible. It all looks a bit like moist leather.

There's a control console in front of it. You take a closer look. Everything is labelled. 'T-rex Musculature Robot'. Robot? Is it more advanced than the animatronics? There's a clearly labelled ON switch. Perhaps you should give it a go?

To try out the controls,
go to page 63.

If you decide not to, then
go to page 61.

You come out of hiding and introduce yourself to Mr Richly. He does not look happy to see you. But he doesn't speak to you. Instead he turns to glare at Gaspar.

'You led him here,' he growls in a low voice. 'I will deal with you shortly.' Now he finally turns his attention to you. 'But first I need to dispose of this interloper.'

Dispose? That doesn't sound good.

Richly advances on you, brandishing his walking stick. What's he going to do? Clobber you with it? But with a swish, he pulls a concealed sword from the end of it. He continues to advance and you back away.

You back up all the way through the French doors and into the courtyard until you come to the edge of the pond. But Richly continues to advance and you fall backwards over the edge and into the water. It's a lot deeper than it looks, and you have to dog paddle to keep your head above water.

Now what?

You feel something swish past your leg.

What was that?

There's something in the water with you and it's a lot bigger than a goldfish. You begin to panic as you see the water ahead of you ripple. Then the surface breaks as a Dunkleosteus rises up. It's a gigantic, armoured, Devonian-period fish with razor-sharp bony protrusions in its mouth. And it's heading right for you, jaws agape.

CHOMP!

You are prehistoric fish food.

You sit down in the capsule and are immediately whisked away through the glass transport tube. The trees below are streaking by at such a speed. You can see your destination approaching. There are cages with dinosaurs. Are they real?

The tube dips down and leads to a building, where the capsule stops. You disembark and make for the door. You can see Richly and Gaspar heading off in a little vehicle a bit like a golf cart. It's pottering along a path between cages.

The cages are filled with dinosaurs. And they are definitely real! You can see an Aardonyx, an Ankylosaurus, an Apatosaurus – which makes you wonder if they've been arranged in alphabetical order – and a whole bunch of creatures you don't recognise.

You actually feel sorry for the dinosaurs. Each is in an individual cage and each cage only seems barely large enough for its occupant. Is this some sort of private zoo?

You set off at a jog and catch up with Richly as he and Gaspar disembark and approach a railing. You hide behind a tree and peer around it.

You look up to the sky at the sound of approaching helicopters. You see four large twin-rotor transport copters, flying in formation, with something suspended between them. It's a dinosaur in a net. Is it dead? Unconscious? You can't tell what sort it is, but it's BIG! You watch as they lower it towards Richly.

Needing a better vantage point, you climb up into the tree. The helicopters are lowering the dinosaur into a pit surrounded by a low railing. You can tell it's a Spinosaurus by its long crocodile-like snout and the bony 'sail' on its back. It's the longest of the carnivores. As it reaches level with the railing, one of its claws slashes through the netting. It tumbles forward into the pit, its tail thrashing. Looks like it is alive!

Its tail smashes the railing as it falls, narrowly missing Richly but knocking Gaspar off his feet. Richly gazes down into the pit, then back at Gaspar, as the helicopters fly off. The little dinosaur is making distressed, high-pitched sounds as if in pain. Richly approaches him and looks down, leaning heavily on his walking stick.

'What shall we do?' he asks.

Good question. What will you do?

To stay hidden in the tree and watch,
go to page 73.

But Gaspar is hurt. To help,
go to page 71.

You tentatively reach out towards the controls but stop before you actually touch any. You decide it's best not to mess with it. Suddenly, you're startled by a shrill voice from behind.

'What are you doing?'

You spin around, lose your footing and fall back onto the controls, knocking them over. As the controls explode into sparks, the T-rex robot bursts into life. It roars and snaps its jaws before stomping around, its massive feet crushing workbenches beneath them. Its tail narrowly misses the bony T-rex but smashes aside an animatronic Stegosaurus. You quickly run out of the way as it lumbers forward, clearing a path through the workshop. It looks so much worse now that it's moving. It's like an animated lump of meat in the shape of a dinosaur. Why would anyone want to make this?

As you watch, it tears through the side of the workshop and lumbers off towards the Animatronics Park.

'We've gotta stop it!' You spin around again to see a woman in grease-stained overalls. She's got a mop of curly white hair and a determined expression. 'Come with me,' she says, running in the opposite direction to the dinosaur.

What do you do?

To follow the strange woman,
go to page 67.

To follow the T-rex,
go to page 80.

You tentatively reach out and press the ON button for the skinless T-rex. You decide to wait and see what happens before switching on the skeletal version.

Slowly the T-rex comes to life in all its meaty glory – its head swinging from side to side, its tail swooshing, its useless little arms dog paddling in the air. It gnashes its teeth and gazes down at you with empty eye sockets. It really is super creepy. Its head is beginning to lower, when you're startled by a shrill voice from behind.

'What are you doing?'

You spin round to see a woman in grease-stained overalls marching towards you with a half-eaten ice cream in one hand. She's got a mop of curly white hair and an angry expression. 'For heaven's sake, switch it off. It's not been tested. It could — LOOK OUT!'

You turn just in time to see the T-rex's head, jaws open wide, bearing down on you.

You scream as you are scooped up into its mouth.

You hear a muffled voice in the distance shouting: 'Just relax and go with the flow. I guess we're testing out Rexy's gastrointestinal process.'

You're expecting those teeth to chomp down on you any second . . . but they don't. Instead, the creature's slimy tongue pushes you down into the throat. You find yourself being squeezed and pushed along in complete darkness by the internal muscles, until you are dropped into its stomach. You splash down into a tight space filled with foul-smelling slop. You're gagging, doing your best not to lose your breakfast. But the horror isn't over yet.

As you wallow in the mess, you can feel it being drained away. Then you're again being pulled and pushed and massaged by wet, meaty muscles, down into a narrow tube. You can barely breathe, the smell getting progressively worse as the sludge around you firms up. You continue to be pushed along the seemingly endless winding tube, until . . .

One last squeeze and you find yourself being expelled from the robotic, skinless T-rex as it poops you out onto the floor. You land in the centre of a massive pile of stinky, sticky dinosaur faeces.

You wipe the muck from your face, your eyes streaming and your throat constricting as you splutter and gag. You see a face looking down at you.

'That was incredible!' says the woman with curly hair. She's no longer angry. Her face is alight with enthusiastic joy. 'I designed this robot as a demonstration model of T-rex musculature and of the gastrointestinal system. And you've just proved that it works!'

You wonder why anyone would want to do that.

The woman extends a hand and helps you out of the poo.

'I need you to come with me and make a statement detailing everything that you just experienced. Every sensation that you felt. Smell. Touch. Taste. Everything!'

You're not sure you want to relive that experience.

'And after that,' she continues, 'since you're now an experienced tester, I've got a Giganotosaurus behind the workshop for you to try out.'

WHAT?

You follow the strange woman to a cubicle at the end of the workshop. She grabs a couple of apple-sized devices with rings dangling from their tops and tosses them to you. OMG! Are these grenades?

'They're EMP charges,' the woman says. 'We'll need them to knock out Rexy.'

EMP?

'Electromagnetic pulse,' she explains as she grabs another couple for herself. 'The pulse knocks out all electronics within a ten-metre radius.'

She tucks a plastic tube into her belt and passes you one as well. 'Launcher.' Jamming a cowboy hat onto her head, she leads the way back to the skeletal T-rex. She hits the ON button, then grabs a remote control from the panel.

'Saddle up,' she instructs.

What?

The woman nimbly runs up the tail of the skeleton, onto its back. She motions for you to

follow. You gulp down your fear and climb – your ascent not quite so nimble. There's a saddle for you to sit in and thankfully it has a seatbelt. The woman turns to you and holds out a hand. 'The name's Mavis,' she says, shaking your hand. 'Robotics engineer. Figured I should introduce myself before we head into battle.'

Battle!

'Yippee!' she shouts as she operates the remote control. The skeleton lurches forward and gallops off, with you holding onto the saddle for dear life.

This is utterly surreal! You are chasing a skinned T-rex robot, seated on the back of a skeletal T-rex robot. Can things get any more weird?

As you head out into the Animatronics Park, people run screaming when they see you. Above, a helicopter is skimming down over the trees.

'That'll be security,' cries Mavis. 'We need to hurry up, 'cause they'll just blast poor old Rexy. That's their answer to everything – hit it, shoot it or blow it up.'

The skeleton puts on an extra burst of speed and soon you see the meaty T-rex. It's attacking its animatronic counterpart. Your inner dino nerd knows this is probably because these creatures are supposed to have been territorial. But pride in your knowledge is short-lived, as you notice your friends are down there. Jake is lying on the ground, injured, and Jen is trying to help him up. You come to a stop about fifteen metres from the one-sided fight.

The helicopter is swooping low over the scene. What is Mavis waiting for? Your friends are in danger. Maybe you should take the initiative and launch an EMP charge?

To launch an EMP charge,
go to page 74.

To let Mavis handle things,
go to page 82.

You jump down from your hiding place and run over.

'Who are you and what are you doing here?' demands Richly.

Does it matter? You just want to help with Gaspar.

'Very well,' says Richly. 'Pick it up and bring it over here.'

Gaspar whimpers as you pick him up, and you stumble a little as you get used to the weight. You join Richly at the edge of the pit where the railing has been smashed away. Now what?

'Even injured, it can serve a purpose,' says Richly, eyes cold and calculating. 'Into the pit.'

What? No, you can't do that.

'I would like to see my new pet's capabilities,' explains Richly. 'Plus, it needs to be fed. So if you won't oblige, I shall have to prompt you.'

Quick as a flash, he pokes you with his walking stick. You teeter on the edge, desperately

hanging onto the injured dinosaur . . . then into the pit you both go. Thankfully, the fall knocks you unconscious, so you don't have to experience being eaten alive.

You stay hidden and watch.

Richly takes hold of Gaspar's tail, dragging him to the edge of the pit where the railing has been smashed away. OMG! He's going to throw the dinosaur into the pit. You have to do something. You jump down from the tree and yell at him to STOP!

But you are too late!

Over the edge, Gaspar goes. You can hear a roar from the Spinosaurus.

Richly is now staring at you with a shocked expression. 'Who the blazes are you?' He quickly recovers his composure, his eyes hardening, his voice becoming demanding. 'Come here this instant and explain yourself!'

What will you do?

To approach Richly, go to page 75.

To run away, go to page 77.

As the chopper passes over the dinosaurs, you pop the EMP charge into the launcher tube and fire.

But at that moment the skinless Rexy tears one of the arms off the animatronic dinosaur with its mouth and spits it out. As your EMP device flies through the air, it hits the arm and is propelled high up over you . . . right where the helicopter is flying.

The EMP charge emits its burst of electro-magnetic radiation. Rexy is out of range now and shifts its attack to Jake and Jen. But the helicopter gets the full blast. Its engine cuts out, its rotors slow and the whole thing drops out of the sky . . .

Right on to you and Mavis atop the skeleton.

KA-BOOM!

You march over to the old man, ranting about how cruel and inhuman he is.

'If you are so concerned about the Gasparinisaura,' he says, stepping towards you, swinging his walking stick, 'perhaps you should join it in feeding my new pet.'

Quick as a flash he pulls a concealed sword from his walking stick and has it at your throat. He leads you to the edge of the pit.

'In you go,' he says as he lunges.

But you dodge out of the way.

Richly stumbles forward to the precipice. You think he's about to go over, but he steadies himself. Within seconds, his sword is aimed at you again. 'Don't make this harder than it has to be,' he sneers. 'And don't think of running. If you do, I'll simply release my Deinonychus. It's one of the Cretaceous period's most accomplished hunters. And I've trained it to track and eat whoever I tell it to.'

It seems like there's no escape.

But then you see something snaking its way out from the pit. It's a tail! The tail swipes at Richly's feet. The man loses his balance and drops his sword as he windmills his arms, teetering on the edge. But he's fighting a losing battle with gravity. Finally, as if in slow motion, he pitches over the side, his scream echoing up from the depths of the pit. He's Spinosaurus food!

You race to the edge to see Gaspar clinging to a broken piece of railing that was bent over the side when the Spinosaurus attempted escape. You lie on your stomach, lean over and grab onto the little dinosaur, pulling him to safety. The poor thing has a broken leg, so you pick him up and carry him back to the transport tube.

You return to the workshop and ask for Mavis's help.

Go to page 155.

You turn and run!

'My pets will get you!' you hear Richly shouting. 'You won't escape!'

Maybe not . . . but you're going to give it a darn good try. As you race to the transport tube you hear the sounds of pursuit. But then the sounds are gone. You run on, feeling hopeful. But as you approach the building with the tube entrance you see that your escape is blocked. Standing in front of the door is a vicious-looking feathered dinosaur with massive claws and sharp, backwards-curving teeth. Deinonychus is about a head taller than you and the perfect killing machine. It must have circled around and overtaken you.

The sound of an approaching vehicle makes you turn. It's Richly in his golf cart. And he's got two more dinosaurs following him, a Velociraptor and another species of raptor. They are smaller than the Deinonychus but look just as dangerous. And they begin to stalk towards you.

But why? Why are they hunting you and not Richly?

'I've trained them,' explains Richly, holding up a small device. 'Each of them has an electrified collar.' He activates the device and the three dinosaurs fall to the ground, writhing in pain. 'They know not to disobey me.'

Now's your chance. While the dinosaurs are recovering from their shock therapy, you launch yourself at Richly. You try to wrestle the device from his grip but there's a strap that he's looped around his wrist. Not knowing what else to do, you slam his hand and the device into the side of cart. Richly yelps in pain as the device falls to pieces.

'What are you doing?' yells Richly. His voice has raised a notch and his eyes have widened. 'They'll attack both of us.'

As if to give weight to his words, the three dinosaurs are now advancing towards the two of you. Richly backs away but you just close your eyes, accepting your fate. There's nothing more you can do.

At Richly's piercing scream, your eyes snap open. The three creatures are ignoring you and attacking him. You guess they're out for revenge.

You take the opportunity to dash for the transport tube. Soon, you're back at the workshop telling Mavis everything that has happened.

Go to page 155.

You have no idea who that woman is. There's no way you're following her. You take off after the dinosaur instead. As you run through the workshop you look for anything that might be able to help you. Are those fireworks? You're not sure but you grab a couple of them anyway. You also snatch up a hand-held blowtorch, then continue on.

You follow the robot's path of destruction back to the Animatronics Park. There is utter chaos as students and teachers are yelling and running about in hysterics. The security guards are doing little more than panicking themselves.

You eventually catch up with the skinless T-rex as it attacks its animatronic counterpart. Your inner dino nerd knows this is probably because these creatures are supposed to have been territorial. But pride in your knowledge is short-lived, as you notice your friends, Jake and Jen. Jake is injured and Jen is trying to help him. Overhead, a helicopter comes swooping down, flying low over the scene.

The meaty robot rips off one of the animatronic's arms with its mouth and spits it out. It lands right in front of you, looking even more useless than when it was attached.

The robot turns its attention to your friends. You've got to do something to help them.

To light the fireworks in the hope of distracting the robot from your friends, go to page 86.

To attack the robot with the blowtorch, go to page 84.

You are itching to launch an EMP charge and save your friends, but you figure you'd better leave it to Mavis. She seems to know what she's doing.

As the chopper passes over the dinosaur, you shout at Mavis to do something.

'Can't use the EMP,' she calls. 'Those kids down there are too close. Can't risk Rexy falling on 'em.'

The skinless creature tears one of the arms off its animatronic counterpart with its mouth and spits it out into the air. Then it turns its attention to your friends. You know what you have to do.

You unclip your seatbelt and scamper down the bony tail. (Actually, it's more of an uncoordinated tumble with a thump at the end. But let's not quibble.) You race to your friends, helping Jen to lift Jake up off the ground. He's hurt his leg, but between the two of you, you manage to get him moving . . . just in time! Rexy's massive, muscled foot comes down on the exact spot where Jake had been lying.

As the three of you get out of the way, you shout at Mavis. She launches an EMP charge just as Rexy opens its mouth wide in a ferocious roar. The EMP flies into its open mouth and emits its burst of electromagnetic radiation.

Rexy freezes. Teeters. And then comes crashing to the ground, completely taking out the animatronic.

You and your friends are safe!

But Rexy has caused an awful lot of damage. Maybe it should be renamed from T-rex to T-wrecks? You grin at your own joke. But is this really the time to be making jokes? After all, someone is going to be blamed for all this. And that someone is YOU!

You charge at the skinless T-rex robot with the blowtorch, setting fire to the muscles on its leg. You have no idea what the muscles are made of, but whatever it is, it's flammable. The entire creature ignites in a whoosh of flames and you get a sudden whiff that reminds you of your dad's barbequing. But you've got no time to be hungry, because the danger is far from over.

The flaming meat dino staggers back, away from your friends. You run over to them and assist Jake. Between you and Jen, you are able to help him up off the ground to the shelter of nearby trees.

The flames have not stopped the robot. It is now more horrific than ever. It's a mass of burning muscles and tendons rampaging around the park, setting alight everything and anything it comes into contact with.

As the helicopter does another fly-by, the flaming T-rex rears its head, opens its jaws and

chomps the chopper out of the sky. Flaming debris rains down, setting fire to the trees you're sheltering under.

As the creature stomps off towards the Research and Education Centre, leaving smouldering footprints in its wake, alarms start blaring. A voice over the PA system announces an evacuation, urging everyone to head for the ferries.

As you and your friends are running, you catch a glimpse of the other robot T-rex, the skeletal one. It looks as if someone is riding it, chasing after the flaming meaty one. The strain of everything that's happened must be getting to you. You're imagining things.

The three of you make your way to the dock. As your ferry pulls away, you and your class watch the island burn!

You just hope no one realises that it's all your fault! Especially not Mr Hendrickson, 'cause he'd definitely give you extra homework.

To use the blowtorch you'd have to get really close to the robot and you don't want to do that. So fireworks it is!

You light the fuse on one of the fireworks with the blowtorch, then you toss it to one side of the skinless T-rex. You hope it will attract the robot's attention, giving Jake and Jen a chance to escape.

But rather than getting fabulously colourful bursts of brilliant brightness, what you get is a massive explosion. The blast almost knocks the robot off its feet and onto your friends. But it regains its balance just in time, turning its meaty face to you. You see Jake and Jen stagger slowly away.

You glance at the second firework that you're holding and realise that what you actually picked up were sticks of dynamite. Oh well, you've got to work with what's at hand.

You light the second stick and wait for the fuse to burn down. As the robot dinosaur opens its jaws to roar, you toss the stick into its mouth and RUN!

KA-BOOM!

The robot dinosaur's head explodes, sending pieces of machinery and synthetic meaty bits in all directions. The body teeters then falls, crushing the animatronic T-rex.

At that moment you see an incredible sight. The robotic T-rex skeleton from the workshop comes galloping along. And atop the robot, riding it like a horse, is that strange woman with the curly white hair. Bringing the robot to a halt, she nimbly runs down its skeleton tail as if it were merely a set of steps and charges up to you.

'What the heck have you done?' she demands, surveying the wreckage. 'You've destroyed my musculature robot *and* my T-rex animatronic. You are in BIG trouble.'

You head off to the Research and Education Centre. From the entrance foyer, there are multiple doorways leading to a rabbit warren of corridors. You and the other students are met by a young man in a lab coat. He's got wide, excitable eyes and long blond hair tied back into a neat ponytail.

'Hey there. I'm Cody,' he introduces himself. 'I'm a student lab assistant in the DNA department, but today I'm going to be your tour guide.' He punches the air enthusiastically. 'Yay me!' You and the other students don't respond.

Really? A student lab assistant? You were hoping for a real scientist. There are lots of them about. You notice some of them have a security pass around their necks. Hmmm. Cody doesn't have one of those.

'Today, I'm gonna take you on a tour of the DNA labs and explain some of the work that we're doing here.' He points to the doorway

marked 'DNA Research'. 'Please note that there are several restricted areas, so don't go wandering. Stick close to me.'

He then indicates a doorway to the left. 'After the tour, you can take a walk through the palaeontology exhibition. We have a number of real dinosaur skeletons on display. There will be a palaeontologist there to answer any questions you may have.'

Dinosaur bones! Now that sounds way more interesting.

'Now, if you will all follow me, we can get things started.' Tour Guide Cody leads the way past the DNA research sign and down a corridor. But do you follow? The palaeontology exhibition sounds more interesting. So does exploring on your own. But the disapproving face of Mr Hendrickson looms in your mind's eye, telling you to stick with the tour. Do you?

To go on the tour with Cody,
go to page 99.

To skip the tour and go straight
to the dinosaur bones, go to page 97.

To be really naughty and sneak off into one
of the Staff Only areas, go to page 102.

You wait in line for the VR game. It takes AGES before it's finally your turn.

But as you get ready to climb into the pod, a student from another school slips in front of you and enters it.

'You snooze, you lose,' he says with a chuckle.

You are livid! You grab the guy and try to pull him out of the pod. But he's already put on the helmet. As you yank him out of it, all the wiring connected to the helmet is ripped out.

The two of you are in big trouble. The staff fetch your teachers. You don't know what happens to the other kid, but you are escorted by a furious Mr Hendrickson back to the ferry that brought you and your fellow students to the island. And there you wait, all alone, as everyone else gets to enjoy the rest of the day.

Tough luck!

It's a long line and you don't have the patience to wait. So you saunter over to the dark corner of the Welcome Lounge and sidle up to the game pod. You take the sign and drop it behind the machine, out of view. Then you climb into the pod and put on the special helmet.

You are presented with a menu:

- Dynamic Dinosaur Experience (public)
- Files (staff only)

Do you take a look at the staff-only files? Or do you play the game?

To take a look at the files, go to page 95.

But really, they're probably full of boring stuff like research. To go straight for the game, go to page 93.

You load up the game and are immediately immersed in a world of dinosaurs, excitement and adventure. What you don't realise is that, while providing you with lots of thrills and spills, the game is also teaching you about the prehistoric environment. Education disguised as entertainment. Whatever will they think of next?

You are so engrossed that you don't keep track of the time. It is many hours later that a heavy hand falls on your shoulder and you are yanked out of the game.

Your teacher is furious! You have never seen Mr Hendrickson so angry. His face is a particularly vivid shade of red and the vein in his temple is pulsing so energetically you're worried it might actually burst. The excursion finished an hour ago and the entire class has been searching for you. You have held up the ferry . . . and so also the bus waiting on the mainland to take you back to school . . . and therefore also all the parents coming to collect their kids at the appointed time.

Detentions, extra homework and a grounding await you on your return. If only you could have stayed in the VR past. Those prehistoric perils seem so much more manageable than the consequences of your decisions.

You can't help yourself. You're curious. You select Files. You are greeted by the following submenu:

- Subterranean palaeontological dig
- Newly discovered species
- DNA extraction database
- Cloning results
- Hybrid species experiments
- Time travel

Whoa!

This is much more than you were expecting. But which will you choose?

To choose Subterranean palaeontological dig, go to page 233.

To choose Newly discovered species, go to page 233.

To choose DNA extraction database,
go to page 233.

To choose Cloning results,
go to page 233.

To choose Hybrid species experiments,
go to page 233.

To choose Time travel,
go to page 233.

You enter the palaeontology exhibition and your eyes light up. It is amazing!

You are in a massive space with a high domed ceiling. There is a Pterosaur skeleton suspended from the centre, with a spiral staircase leading up to it so people can get a closer look. Display cases are dotted amongst numerous full skeletons.

Your eye is immediately drawn to the Brachiosaurus on your right, as it dominates the room with its size. But to your left is a Velociraptor display with five skeletons set out as if they're all hunting together. Which should you go to first?

To check out the Brachiosaurus skeleton,
go to page 104.

If you'd rather see the raptors,
go to page 113.

You follow Tour Guide Cody and the school group down the corridor. As you go, he explains about DNA, or deoxyribonucleic acid. It's a tiny molecule that contains genetic code that is unique to every living organism. 'Basically,' he concludes, 'it's kinda like an instruction manual for creating whatever organism it comes from.'

You enter a large laboratory. There are people in lab coats at long benches working with test tubes and syringes and various bits of high-tech equipment.

'So, this is where we search for dino DNA,' says Cody. 'No, we don't get it from amber-encased mosquitoes like in that silly dinosaur film. There are a number of different ways in which we acquire it. The simplest is . . . if dinosaur cartilage has been preserved in just the right way, it will sometimes contain a tiny skerrick of DNA. But that minuscule bit is all we need to start piecing together what that dinosaur would have been.'

Next, he leads you into a room full a people seated at computers. 'In here, we analyse that DNA and begin to create computer generated models of the dinosaurs.' He points to a door at the other end of the room. 'From here it's then just a hop, skip and jump to cloning.'

'Couldn't that be dangerous?' calls out one student.

'Yeah,' says another. 'What if you clone a T-rex and then it eats you!' Everyone laughs.

'That's not gonna happen,' says Cody with a grin. 'Firstly, we are waaaaay off being able to actually clone a living dinosaur. We are just in the early stages of cloning individual cells. And we have strict guidelines to only experiment with small herbivores.'

While Cody's been talking, you've been looking over the shoulder of one of the computer operators. Your eyes widen at the information that flickers across his screen. You see a diagram of a DNA pattern that's labelled 'Spinosaurus'. You focus in on the words 'cloning status'.

You're pretty sure that the Spinosaurus was a large, vicious carnivore. Are they trying to clone one? Has Cody been lying about the research being conducted here? Should you ask him about it?

To confront Cody about what you just saw on the computer screen, go to page 108.

But that would be rude, wouldn't it? To ignore what you saw and continue the tour uninterrupted, go to page 106.

You head off through one of the doorways with a 'Staff Only' sign. Walking along the corridor, you're trying your best to look as if you belong there. Thankfully there doesn't seem to be anyone around. You pass several locked doors with 'Restricted Area' signs. You wish you could get a look inside one of these.

The corridor leads you to an office area. Boring! You were hoping for something a little more interesting. Most of the area is open plan, with shoulder-height partitions dividing the area into small cubicles. The people at the desks are all concentrating on their computer screens. You keep close to the wall, trying to make sure you're not in anyone's line of sight.

There are a few closed-in offices. You peer through the little glass panel on the door to the first one. There's a desk with a computer, some chairs and an old-fashioned filing cabinet. But what really catches your attention is a pegboard on the far wall. Hanging on that board are a number of those security passes you've seen some of the staff wearing around their necks. If you could get one of those you might be able to get access to some more interesting places.

You look around. No one is watching you. You could slip into the office and borrow a pass. But should you?

To enter the office, go to page 110.

To continue around the open-plan area and explore what's beyond, go to page 160.

You walk towards the Brachiosaurus skeleton, your mouth hanging open. It's so big, the neck curving up high, its head almost level with the hanging Pterosaur.

You glance quickly to the information sign beside it. It gives you all the standard info – Jurassic period; herbivore; 12 metres tall; 23 metres in length; over 28,000 kg (equivalent to about four African elephants). You know all of this stuff already.

You go right up to the rope barrier to get a closer look at it. This is so cool! The skeletons at your local museum, which you've been to many times, are all reproductions. But this skeleton is genuine! You lean over the barrier to get an even closer look. And that's when you see it . . .

One of the bones looks wrong!

It's in one of the rear feet. There's a bone in the top part of the foot that's sitting at an odd angle. It looks like it's been bumped out of place.

You have a momentary panic, wondering if the entire display is about to collapse on to you.

But it's not falling. It seems to be quite stable. You look around for someone to tell. But it's just kids from the other schools wandering about. Maybe you should fix it?

To climb over the barrier and straighten up the bone, go to page 111.

To ignore it and move on to look at the raptors, go to page 113.

You keep silent about what you saw on the screen. Seconds later it's gone anyway, the screen now showing the DNA profile of Protoceratops, a small herbivore.

As Cody leads everyone back out into the corridor, you begin to question what you saw. Perhaps you misread it? Maybe you imagined it? It doesn't really matter, does it? I mean, it's so unlikely. You should pay attention to the tour.

You walk past a number of doors marked 'Restricted Access'. Every now and then, a scientist will tap a pass onto the sensor by one of these doors and enter. You notice that only a few of the people working here seem to have these passes on lanyards around their necks.

'We're now gonna take a gander at the DNA cloning facility,' says Cody, bringing your attention back to the tour.

You all stop by a large window looking into a lab. All the people working inside it are wearing protective suits and hoods. One of the suited scientists comes to the window and holds up a test tube containing a clear liquid.

'Inside that test tube,' explains Cody, 'is a single cloned cell from a Leaellynasaura. It is our most successful cloning attempt thus far. Not quite sci-fi, is it?'

As Cody continues to provide commentary on what's happening in the lab, you see a scientist entering one of those restricted areas. As the door swings back, you realise you have just enough time to get to it before it closes. You are burning with curiosity – desperate to find out what's in there. What do you do?

To sprint for the door,
go to page 115.

But that would be naughty,
wouldn't it? To stay with the group,
go to page 114.

You point at the computer screen and ask why there's carnivore DNA on it.

'What?' yelps Cody, his eyes wide like a rabbit caught in the headlights of an oncoming car. 'You must be mistaken.'

You look back at the screen, but it's changed. It's now showing a Protoceratops.

'Yeah, look,' he says, his voice high and squeaky. 'That's a herbivore, not a carnivore. Yeah, defs a herbivore. A nice small one at that.' His voice is coming down to a normal pitch again, but you can see that he's sweating and his eyes are darting all over the place. The computer operators are all glaring at him.

'And . . . you know, the thing is . . .' He's babbling now. 'We do sometimes study carnivores as well. Yes. Of course we do. We study all sorts of dinosaurs here. We're like . . . research scientists. It's what we do. It's just that only the small herbivore DNA is used for the cloning experiments. I mean, yeah, why would we use anything else. That'd be, like . . . stupid and dangerous and unethical and probably illegal and . . . Oh, look at the time.' He points to the clock on the wall and then makes a beeline for the door. 'I think we've used up all our time. Yep. Abso-defs! Outta time. Follow me. Chop chop!'

He leads you back out and quickly disappears. Now what?

To check out the palaeontology exhibition, go to page 97.

Or, maybe you could sneak into one of the Staff Only areas and explore? Go to page 160.

You try the door. It isn't locked so you slip into the office. You don't bother looking around; you head straight for the pegboard. You smile and snatch one of the passes.

But your smile doesn't last, as an alarm blares.

You pocket the pass and dash to the door. Looking through the glass you see a security guard enter the office area and head towards you. You take a deep breath, open the door and step out.

Now what do you do?

To stay and try to talk your way out of it, go to page 119.

To run, go to page 121.

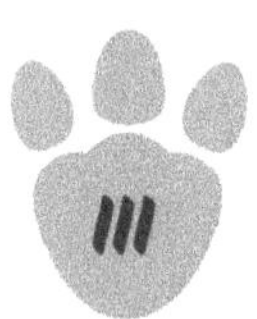

You climb over the barrier and crouch down beside the Brachiosaurus's rear legs. You reach out for the bone in its foot.

'NO!' The shout comes from behind you. 'Don't touch it!'

You look over your shoulder to see a man in a tweed jacket rushing towards you. 'I'm Professor Calcifeir, head palaeontologist. And you can't just go around touching the exhibits. These bones are priceless!'

You step away from the Brachiosaurus and explain that you were just trying to fix the bone. You point it out to Prof Calcifeir.

He squints at the dinosaur's foot through his round glasses. 'Oh, I see,' he says. 'It's still not a good idea for you to go touching exhibits. You could easily cause irreparable damage. These things are best left to the professionals.' He grins at you. 'Like me!

'Fear not,' he continues, 'I shall take care of this. You run along and enjoy the rest of the exhibition.'

He's a little bit condescending, isn't he?

As he steps over the barrier, you shrug and head off towards the raptor display. You're halfway there when you notice a small bone lying on the floor. You are about to pick it up when you hear a yell from behind. You whirl around.

Prof Calcifeir is backing away from the Brachiosaurus skeleton, which is swaying precariously above him. OMG! It's going to fall! That's a sight you don't see every day. So much for the professor being an expert.

As the Brachiosaurus collapses, people scream and run. A few of the kids stop to video the incident on their phones. Viral internet fame probably awaits them.

You figure it's best to get out of there, just in case Prof Calcifeir decides to blame you. You race out the door and head towards the Welcome Lounge. Maybe you could have another go at the VR game.

Go to page 31.

You head towards the Velociraptor exhibit. As you are walking towards it, you notice something lying on the floor. You crouch down for a better look.

It's a small bone. You pick it up and examine it more closely.

Could it be a dinosaur bone?

You look around. Is it from one of the exhibits? Could you perhaps put it back where it belongs? It would be a bit like solving a mystery.

To try to find the exhibit it belongs to, go to page 122.

But it might be better to just hand it in to someone who works here. To do that, go to page 133.

Cody's spiel continues. 'The next step will be to see if we can use that cell to grow an embryo.'

You're finding this a bit boring and your mind quickly begins to wander. You gaze around. There's a group of scientists bustling along the corridor. Your tour group has to squeeze up to let them pass.

As they go by, one of them drops his security pass. It practically falls at your feet, begging you to pick it up. You quickly bend down and snaffle it. This pass could get you through the doors marked 'Restricted Access'. In fact, it could probably get you into all sorts of interesting places.

But what do you do with it?

To stick the pass into your pocket and keep it, go to page 123.

To give it back to the scientist who dropped it, go to page 117.

While the tour group is preoccupied looking through the window, you sprint for the door. You catch it just in time and slip into a short passage. You see the scientist disappear through the opening at the other end. Slowly, you creep along after her.

Up ahead you can see glass boxes. You wonder what that's all about. But as you get closer you realise that the boxes are incubators and that there are really big eggs inside each of them. And you're pretty sure that they are dinosaur eggs.

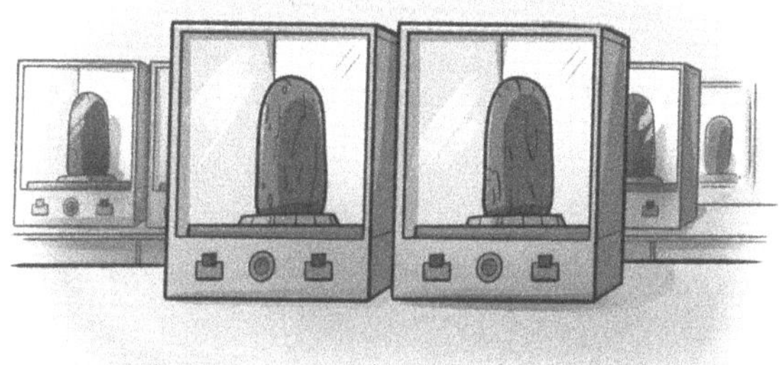

You take a moment to goggle at them before continuing on.

The next room is filled with rows of stacked enclosures. In each, there is a live baby dinosaur. Your mouth is now hanging open, your brain barely able to cope with what you are seeing. As you walk along one aisle, your eyes move from one baby dino to the next. You don't recognise all the species, but you certainly know that at least two of them are types of raptors. And raptors are carnivores. Cody was lying to you and the tour group!

You hear footsteps behind you and turn to see the scientist round the corner from the aisle to the left. She's carrying a baby dinosaur. It might be a Stegosaurus. She looks up and sees you.

You stare at her. She stares at you. You yelp. She gasps.

She's between you and the exit. What do you do?

To run in the opposite direction,
go to page 125.

To pretend you are lost,
go to page 127.

You chase after the scientist and hand him back his pass.

'Oh my goodness,' says the scientist. 'How ridiculously careless of me. I would have been in big trouble if an unauthorised person had used it to get into a restricted area.' You note the fear in his voice.

He waves the other scientists off and turns back to you. 'I'm Dr Martin. I specialise in the bones of dinosaur feet. I guess you could say that I'm a palaeontological podiatrist.' He grins and looks expectantly at you, as if he's said something incredibly funny. Then he puts a sudden hand on your shoulder. 'You need to come with me. Right now!'

He takes you straight to the gift shop and tells you to pick whatever you like, then races off. You browse the shelves and end up choosing a plush T-rex and a model of a Triceratops skeleton. By the time you've made your choice, he's back with a free family pass to the Dynamic Dinosaur Discovery Complex, an invitation to the gala grand opening celebration in two weeks' time and the promise of a personal tour for you and your family when you come back.

Wow!

All this just for being honest!

You try to smile as the security guard approaches.

Your smile falters a little as you get a good look at the guard. She is enormous – really tall, with broad shoulders and a thick neck. She looks like she could snap you in two. She's got a shaved head and a mean look on her face.

'You'd better have one heck of an explanation for being here, kid,' she demands.

Your mouth is suddenly dry as sandpaper and you swallow hard. Your voice is all squeaky with nerves as you tell her that you got lost while trying to find the toilets. It's obvious that she doesn't believe you . . . especially once she finds the pass in your pocket.

Taking you by the elbow, she escorts you back to your teacher. Mr Hendrickson is furious with you. He puts you in a small waiting room, telling you to write an essay on why it is essential to follow instructions when on a school excursion.

Writing an essay while everyone else is enjoying themselves is the last thing you want to do. Perhaps you could sneak out to play the VR game again. But if you get caught you'd end up in even more trouble.

To play it safe, stay put and write the essay, go to page 50.

To go back to the VR game, go to page 31.

You bolt!

Jumping over desks and clambering over partitions, you aim for the far side of the area. The security guard is huge, but not very agile. You manage to make it without getting caught. But as you run through a doorway into a rabbit warren of corridors, you hear the guard blowing on a whistle. Soon there are multiple guards chasing you . . . and they're gaining.

You pass several doors, but each time you stop to try one, it's locked. The guards are now so close you can't risk stopping to try any more doors. So you keep running.

Up ahead the corridor splits in two. Which way will you go? Right or left?

To turn right, go to page 150.

To turn left, go to page 154.

You decide to solve the mystery of the bone. The Velociraptor exhibit is the closest, so you walk over to it. Heading to the first of the raptor skeletons, you hold up the bone to compare. The one you're holding is a lot cleaner and whiter than those in the raptor. You lean in to examine the display a little closer.

'What are you doing?' comes a shout from behind.

You whirl around to see a man in a tweed jacket rushing towards you. Your heart jumps into your mouth. What should you do?

Your first instinct is to run away. To do so, go to page 132.

But surely it would be more sensible to simply explain what you're doing? To do that, go to page 136.

You would love to get a look in one of the restricted areas. So you slip the security pass into your pocket and continue the tour. You justify your actions by blaming the clumsy scientist. It's his fault for dropping it at your feet.

As the tour ends you are greeted with an unexpected sight.

An explosion of black curls in a yellow jumpsuit comes bustling into the DNA area, followed by an entourage of people with cameras and flashing phones. You rub your eyes as she approaches and stops. She is wearing her signature pink tiara. It's Jasmine Lesaale, or Princess Jazzy as she calls herself online, the self-proclaimed Princess of Social Media. She's a super-famous, mega-rich, big-time influencer. What in the world is she doing here?

She holds up a hand to silence her gaggle of hangers-on. 'Enough! I need alone time now. You may all scoot.' Her entourage immediately backs out of the corridor.

She smiles and waves as she passes your group. Further along the corridor she holds a pass up to one of the 'Restricted Area' doors. It opens and she slips in. Why does she have a pass? What's behind that door?

You want to follow her straight away. But you wait patiently until the tour group disperses and you're alone. You slip back down the corridor.

Now . . . which 'Restricted Area' door was it that she went in? You're pretty sure it was one of those on the left. But was it the first or the second?

To try the first, go to page 139.

To try the second, go to page 135.

You turn and run.

'Stop!' the scientist calls after you.

You don't stop. You race along the aisle and into the next room. There are cages in here. Cages with bigger dinosaurs. You don't stop to look. You continue running. There's a corridor at the other end. As you reach it, an alarm blares. You continue on.

A door slides into place behind you, blocking the exit. You now have no option but to go on. Up ahead you can see greenery. Does this corridor lead outside? Is this your escape route?

You put on an extra burst of speed and run out into a forested area. Another door slides into place behind you, blocking off the corridor you ran through. You look up. There's no sky! Just a really high ceiling, painted blue with fluffy white clouds around the edges. Nice detail, you think, as you realise you're still inside the Centre.

Why would they have an indoor forest?

ROAAAAAR!

You freeze as a massive reptilian head rears up over the treetops. OMG . . . this is just like the VR game you played at the start of the day. Only this time it's REAL! And it isn't a Giganotosaurus staring down at you. It's actually a Tyrannosaurus rex – the most fearsome predator to ever walk the face of the earth. Once again, your legs feel like jelly and your heart is pounding overtime.

As the T-rex lumbers out of the trees, you back up until you are pressed against the closed door.

There is nowhere for you to go.

It's snack time. And you're the snack!

You smile nervously and wave hello. Taking a deep breath, you launch into an explanation of how you were on a school tour and got lost and how you saw an open door and wandered in thinking it might be a toilet.

The scientist walks towards you, still cradling the baby Stegosaurus. 'There is a huge Restricted Area sign on the door,' she says, frowning at you. 'So, either you can't read or you're lying. I'm sure the security people will be able to figure out which.'

Before you can do anything else, she presses a device on her belt and an alarm blares. Seconds later there are security guards approaching from both directions. You gulp. Your only hope is to cause a distraction. Your eyes dart around furtively, looking for something, anything. You notice that each of the enclosures has a sensor beside it, just like the one beside the door that you came through.

Without any further thought, you spring into action. You snatch the security pass from around the scientist's neck and start tapping it on all the enclosures. Doors slide open and soon baby dinosaurs are all over the place.

You reach into an enclosure to pull out a baby dino. You whisper an apology to it, before tossing it to the guard coming up behind you. Then you dodge around him, going further into the restricted area.

You run into an area filled with cages, but the doorway ahead of you slides closed and two guards come running in after you.

You have no choice . . .

You tap the security pass against the nearest cage. It springs open, releasing a Velociraptor. It's quite small, so it must be an infant. The guards immediately go pale. You run a circuit of the room, tapping the pass as you go, then dodge past the guards as they try to herd the dinosaurs back.

As you run back into the baby dinosaur area, you continue tapping. Pandemonium ensues.

But then you hear a bloodcurdling scream!

You glance back to see the Velociraptor attacking the guards.

And other creatures are venturing out towards you.

Whoops!

You and the scientist run! Back past the eggs, and into the main part of the Centre. Seconds later, there are dinosaurs of all shapes and sizes pouring through the restricted access doorway.

Tour Guide Cody and the students scatter in a panic. More security guards come running. Pretty soon, the entire Centre is in total chaos!

You manage to get out of the Centre, as do the dinosaurs, and back to the ferry that brought you and your class to the island. You don't tell anyone about what you have done. You pretend that you were just as surprised as everyone else to see the real dinosaurs running out all over the place.

Later that night, you watch the news with your family. There's a report about the incident.

The owner of the Dynamic Dinosaur Discovery Complex, Mr Titus B Richly, has been arrested for illegal genetic experiments. The reporter goes on to reveal that investigators also discovered unregistered time travel experiments and wildly unethical genetic experiments involving human beings.

Wow! There was a lot more going on than you realised. You breathe a sigh of relief that you survived it all.

You hope that your next school excursion will be a little more boring. You even vow to follow all of Mr Hendrickson's instructions! Maybe.

Dropping the bone, you bolt!

'Stupid kid!' the man shouts after you, as you run out of the palaeontology exhibition. 'It's just a replica bone from the gift shop!'

What?

You slow to a halt. You suddenly feel rather embarrassed. You've just made a huge scene over a toy bone. You are way too self-conscious to go back into the exhibition. Glancing around, you see all those Staff Only doorways.

You decide to go and explore.

Go to page 102.

You look around for someone official to show what you've found. You spot a man in a tweed jacket going from school group to school group. He seems to be answering questions and directing people where to go. He's probably the best person.

You approach and wait until he's finished explaining about the fossilised shells in one display case to a bunch of bored-looking kids. When he's done, you show him the bone and point to where you found it.

'You can keep it,' he says with a smile.

What? Seriously?

'It's just a replica from the gift shop,' he says. 'I'm really impressed that you decided to hand it in rather than just keep it.'

You explain that you are too interested in palaeontology to not hand it in. After all, it might have been an important artefact.

The man introduces himself as Professor Calcifeir, head palaeontologist. 'I am really

impressed with your attitude,' he says, smiling thoughtfully. 'You say you're interested in palaeontology?'

You nod eagerly.

'Did you know that this Centre is built atop a palaeontological site?'

You shake your head.

'Would you like to see?' he asks enthusiastically. 'Since you're so interested in dinosaur bones, I'd be happy to show you.'

Do you take him up on the offer?

To go with Professor Calcifeir,
go to page 203.

If you'd rather just stick with the exhibit,
go to page 199.

You decide to go for the second door. The coast is clear, so you run for it. Unfortunately, the first door suddenly opens outwards, smashing you in the face.

Your head explodes with pain. Blood gushes from your nose. And you pass out.

You wake up in hospital on the mainland, surrounded by your family. You've been unconscious for almost twenty-four hours. Your hospital room is full of flowers and plush dinosaurs. They've been sent to you as a get-well-soon gift from the Dynamic Dinosaur Discovery Complex, as well as a free family pass for when the park is fully opened.

You are told that you've suffered a concussion and you will need to rest for at least a week. On the bright side, that means you get a week off school. So every cloud has a silver lining.

As the man in the tweed jacket approaches, you hold up the bone you found and explain that you're just trying to find where it belongs.

The man stares at you, then at the bone in your hand, and then back at you. He bursts out laughing. You're rather taken aback. What is so funny?

'That is just a replica bone from the gift shop,' he explains, when he finally stops laughing. 'But thank you for being so conscientious. It is appreciated.' He shakes your hand. 'I'm Professor Calcifeir, head palaeontologist. If you have any questions about the exhibits here, please feel free to ask.'

You're too embarrassed to ask anything. You just shake your head and move off. You take another look at the bone in your hand. It's a fake. What should you do with it?

⋙———→

It could make a nice souvenir of your visit. To keep it, go to Section 71 page 138.

But do you really need a reminder of that embarrassing moment? To chuck it into the bin, go to Section 73 page 142.

You pocket the replica dinosaur bone and continue to look around. It's a really cool exhibition. As well as all the skeletons, there are also display cases with fragments of bones from dinosaurs that have yet to be classified. And there are displays of the equipment that palaeontologists use. There's even fossilised dinosaur poo. It's called a coprolite.

After you are finished, you decide to head back to the Welcome Lounge and have another go at the VR game.

Go to page 31.

You casually stroll down the corridor towards the first door. You are about to use the pass when the door suddenly opens outwards, almost hitting you in the face. A scientist comes rushing out, mumbling something about spoiled internet brats. He's so preoccupied he doesn't notice you. Slamming the door, he strides off. You nonchalantly tap the pass onto the sensor and enter.

There's a blank wall right in front of you. You're momentarily confused until you realise it's there to act as a screen, so no one walking by in the corridor can see what is in here. You cautiously peer around the wall to see a room filled with glass enclosures. And in each one there is a dinosaur. Real, living dinosaurs. But these are unlike any you have ever heard of.

They are all absolutely identical and they are all ridiculously cute. You move closer to examine one of them. It has a round, podgy body and small head with a frilled neck shield. Its eyes are big and round, and it has two tiny blunt horns. The legs are squat but the arms are long. And it's . . . pink!

Princess Jazzy emerges from behind the enclosures carrying one of the cute dinosaurs.

'Who are you?' she asks rudely.

You tell her and she looks down her nose at you. 'If you're not rich and famous, then you shouldn't be in here.'

Why?

She explains that the Cutie-saurs™, as they are apparently called, have been specially created by the DNA scientists here as secret pets for rich and famous people. They cost 1.5 billion dollars each. 'Apparently they need the money to fund other secret experiments,' she concludes. 'I think science is an expensive hobby.' She leans in and whispers, 'I hear they get the dino DNA from prehistory with a time machine.'

You are aghast. You're not even sure how to respond.

'You can't tell anyone,' Jazzy adds, looking suddenly scared. 'If the public found out about this, everyone would want one. And if they were no longer exclusive, then what would be the point?'

You're not sure that's actually the issue here.

'How about I bribe you to keep quiet about this?' she suggests. 'I'll buy you your very own Cutie-saur™.' She smiles at you with dazzlingly white teeth. 'Otherwise they might have to kill you to keep you quiet.' She draws her thumb under her chin in a throat-slitting charade.

Your own secret, genetically manipulated, pet dinosaur? It's tempting!

To accept Princess Jazzy's offer,
go to page 195.

To reject her offer,
go to page 225.

You decide to get rid of the bone, so look around for a bin. There's one to the side of the Velociraptor display. Time to practise your basketball skills.

You take aim and toss the bone. It's heading right for the bin. You're about to pump the air with your fist, but the bone hits the edge of the bin . . .

It rebounds into the air, heading towards the nearest raptor skeleton. You gasp!

The bone hits the raptor's tail. You watch in horror-filled anticipation as the skeleton trembles. For a moment you think that everything's going to be okay. But then the skeleton collapses with a crash into a pile of bones . . .

Except for one bone, which goes skidding across the floor towards the next raptor. Everyone in the exhibition is now staring at you and the raptors as that stray bone knocks into the foot of the second raptor. It teeters,

then falls into the next raptor, which then falls onto the next.

You watch in dumbstruck amazement as skeletons fall like dominos, each one knocking into the next. The crash of each collapsing skeleton echoes around the space, repeating over the top of the next in an almost deafening cacophony. Until finally it's the turn of the Brachiosaurus. It seems like it's all happening in torturous slow motion. As the enormous dinosaur falls forward, its skull detaches and flies through the air, striking the ceiling at the exact point where the wires holding up the Pterosaur are connected.

Released from its bonds, the Pterosaur skeleton swoops down across the room before exploding into bone fragments as it hits the far wall . . .

Right where the fire alarm is situated!

The alarm blares. And the fire sprinklers kick in.

It's like a scene from some disaster flick. And there you are, standing in the middle of the devastation, as water rains down on you.

How in the world are you going to explain your way out of this?

You look at Huggie hugging on to you so tightly and you can't bear to get rid of her. You cuddle her protectively and walk to meet the police. They are astounded by Huggie. And they want to know where you got her.

You decide you can't tell them the truth. After all, you did sign a non-disclosure agreement. So you make up a story about how you found her in the nature reserve and she followed you out.

The police take you home and tell your parents they have to pay for the damage you caused at the convenience store. They are super angry with you but are entranced by Huggie.

Next morning there are reporters at your front door. Someone at the convenience store filmed you and Huggie on their phone. That video has since gone viral on the internet.

You and Huggie appear on the news that night and immediately start getting requests from television chat shows. The two of you quickly become famous . . . and rich!

You now have enough money to ensure Huggie will have as much cat food as she'll ever want. You even get a text message from Princess Jazzy because you are finally *someone*. (You don't respond.)

You and Huggie live happily ever after.

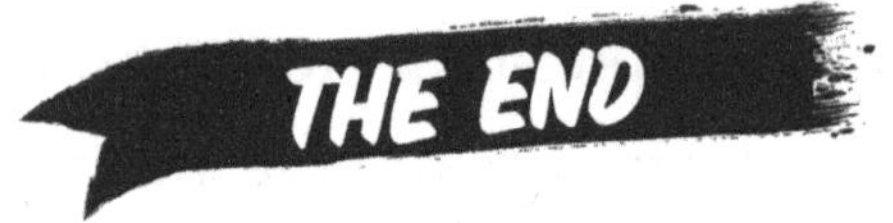

You look at Huggie holding on to you so tightly and your heart almost breaks. But you've got no choice. You have to release her into the wild. It's for her own good.

You disentangle yourself from the Cutiesaur™ and place her on the ground in front of the nature reserve. She looks up at you with her big round eyes. You try to explain things to her, knowing that she can't really understand you, and then give her a little nudge.

She scampers into the undergrowth.

The police arrive and want to know what happened to the strange creature you were seen with. You tell them that you have no idea what it was or where it went – that you'd never seen it before it jumped up onto your backpack in the convenience store. And that you ran away because it frightened you.

The police are sceptical, but they've got no evidence to the contrary, so they take you home.

Your parents are super angry that you snuck out at night.

'Do you realise how dangerous that was?' says your mum.

You end up getting grounded for weeks.

On the plus side, because no one could prove that the creature was yours, you don't have to pay for the damage at the convenience store.

But you miss Huggie very badly. Every time there are stories about stolen supplies of cat food near the nature reserve, you wonder if it's her.

You never see her again.

But . . .

Years later, you come across a news article . . .

THE WOODLEY PHANTOM

What lurks within the trees of Woodley Nature Reserve? Beast or ghost? Friend or foe?

For years there have been legends of the Woodley Phantom, a mysterious creature that haunts a little-known suburban nature reserve. There have been many sightings, with nature lovers,

environmentalists and rangers having close encounters. But the exact nature of the beast is something that no one can agree upon. Theories abound!

There are those who are convinced that it is some sort of large feline, given that the surrounding area is known for the frequent unexplained disappearance of cat food in large quantities. A species not native to the area, such as a panther or wild cat. Perhaps even a hitherto thought-to-be-extinct specimen or a new species altogether.

Others believe it is something of supernatural origin – a ghost, ghoul or spectre.

Perhaps the most outlandish theory is that it's an escaped genetically modified dinosaur. How ridiculous is that!

Whatever it is, locals are convinced that it is benevolent. 'Leave it alone,' advises local resident Belvedere Bradford, 'and it will leave you alone.'

The article brings a smile to your face.

You go right. And you're in a short corridor that ends with a door. You are going so fast that you can't stop in time, slamming into it. You frantically try the handle, but it's locked.

It's a dead end and you're caught. It's all over. Or is it?

The guards catch up, ready to grab you and drag you away.

But the door suddenly opens and a face appears. The guards stop advancing. They're all looking a bit nervous as an elderly lady emerges. She's short, with greying hair and a happy face lined with many wrinkles. She's wearing a stained lab coat over a brown cardigan and plaid floor-length skirt. She has square, wire-rimmed glasses and knitted fingerless gloves.

'It's okay,' she says to the guards. 'I'll look after the kid.'

'But Doc —' starts one of the guards.

'I said I'd look after the kid,' snaps the lady,

her eyes turning to steel. 'You can all go. And there's no need to report this. Understand?'

The guards all nod and hurry away. You are shocked at your sudden change of fortune.

'My name is Dr Genomi Spliser,' she says to you. 'But you may call me Gen.' She smiles. She reminds you of your grandmother. 'Now, my dear, won't you come in?'

You enter a laboratory. And it is the freakiest thing you could possibly imagine. Yes, there are test tubes and Bunsen burners and Petri dishes and all those other things you'd expect to find in a chemistry lab. But what grabs your attention, making you goggle in utter disbelief, are all the weird, bizarre creatures.

There are live ones in cages and dead ones suspended in jars of liquid. The one thing that they all have in common is that they seem to be dinosaur versions of everyday animals.

You can't take your eyes away from them. You approach a pair of dino-piglets, porcine snouts protruding from reptilian faces, lifeless eyes staring at you from a jar. You can't even begin to describe the dino-platypus in the next receptacle.

'Not all my experiments have been successful,' says Dr Spliser's cheery voice from behind you. 'Combining disparate species on a genetic level is often more art than science.'

If this is art, it's seriously messed-up art!

You notice a large bowl containing a green fish, its body covered in long spines. It's using little dinosaur arms to dog paddle through the water.

CLUCK! CLUCK!

The sound of chickens brings your attention to the biggest cage in the room. Of course, they're not ordinary chickens. They are half dinosaur, half chook. Chook-osauruses? And they're almost as big as you. Their bright red combs and white feathery wings contrast with the green reptilian skin that covers the rest of them. Their oversized beaks are filled with razor teeth.

'Ah, Beaky and Dotty, my lovelies,' says Dr Spliser. 'Aren't they simply gorgeous?'

No! No, they are not! You turn to face your

host, about to ask why she's doing this. But she starts talking first.

'Now . . . to business,' she says, steepling her fingers and smiling her warm, friendly smile. 'I believe that you've been a wee bit naughty, haven't you? That would be why you were being chased by security?'

You try to answer, but she continues. 'I like naughty people. You see, it means I don't feel guilty about asking them to help me with my research.' She looks at you pointedly, eyes not quite so friendly anymore. 'So . . . would you like to help me?'

No, you most certainly don't want to help her. But if you don't, you're worried she might hand you back to security. Or worse . . . to the Chook-osauruses. What do you do?

To agree to help her, go to page 157.

To refuse, go to page 156.

You go left!

And knock into a passing scientist. The pass that you've stolen, and forgotten about in the chase, falls out of your pocket. You don't stop to pick it up. You run on.

Behind you, you hear the security guards collide with the scientist. After a while, you realise that you are no longer being chased.

Go to page 160.

Due to Richly's death, Mavis reluctantly calls the police. Over the course of investigations, the extent of Richly's illegal activities are revealed – dangerous experiments with cloning, inhumane treatment of the cloned dinosaurs and even unauthorised time travel experiments. The Complex is closed down, the cloned dinosaurs are released, and the island is turned into a dinosaur sanctuary and declared off limits to humans.

You inadvertently become a celebrity. And given what you have had to endure, you are given two million dollars in compensation from Richly's liquidated estate.

You live richly ever after!

You shake your head, refusing to help, and turn to leave. But, not surprisingly, the door is locked.

'Oh, what a pity,' says Dr Spliser, reaching into the pocket of her lab coat. 'I do so prefer if it's voluntary. But, needs must.'

She holds up a syringe filled with liquid and advances.

She's a little old lady, how hard could it be to overpower her? But then again, she is holding a syringe full of goodness-knows-what with a whopping great needle. What will you do?

To try to disarm her, go to page 166.

To release some of the animals to create a distraction, go to page 168.

You reluctantly nod your agreement.

'Lovely,' she says, warmth and friendliness flooding her eyes again. 'I think we shall get along splendidly.'

She places her thumb up against the far wall. A concealed panel slides back. 'This way.'

You hesitantly follow her into the next room. And breathe a sigh of relief. You were expecting more dino-creatures. But there's only one empty cage in the dark corner. The rest of the room is rather clinical in appearance, surfaces clean and shiny. A bench with notes, a computer tablet and models of both dinosaur and human musculature. There's a high-tech hospital bed within a plastic chamber, the lid propped open.

Your eyes dart to the cage as you hear a low growl. It isn't empty after all.

'Reggie doesn't like the light,' explains Dr Spliser.

You step a little closer and see movement in the shadows. A figure suddenly throws itself against the front of the cage, reptilian arms reaching through the bars trying to get at you with sharp claws. It's a dinosaur man! Hunched and scaled, with a raptor-like muzzle and piercing eyes, he's dressed in rags. If the creatures in the previous room were freaky, this one is next level.

'*Homo Raptorius*,' says Dr Spliser. 'My best attempt thus far. But poor old Reggie is regressing. The Ozraptor DNA is taking over. Every day he's more dinosaur and less human.'

You whisper the name. Ozraptor!

'Oh yes, I know,' says Spilser. 'Ozraptors are not technically part of the raptor family. No feathers. But none of my Velociraptor trials worked. The Ozraptor DNA has been better. Which brings me to why you're here. I think I've solved the problem and I need a fresh test subject.'

You whip around to stare at her. She's holding up a syringe and blocking the exit. 'If you wouldn't mind hopping up onto the bed, we can get started.'

OMG! This nutso scientist wants to turn you into a dinosaur. You stare at the syringe in her hand. 'Oh, don't worry,' she says. 'No needles necessary for the process. It's all done with radioactive bombardment. This is just for persuasion.'

Dr Spliser is between you and the door. Your eyes dart around to see if there's anything useful within reach. Maybe you could throw the dinosaur model at the doctor? Then you remember the security pass in your pocket. Perhaps you can use it to release Reggie? What are you going to do?

To use the security pass, go to page 171.

To throw the model, go to page 177.

To give up and do as Dr Spliser asks, go to page 175.

You spend some time exploring the seemingly endless corridors and offices of the Staff Only area. Without a security pass, you can't get into any of the restricted areas. You are burning with curiosity but are starting to get bored with aimless wanderings.

You're about to give up and head to the Animatronics Park when you spot a door marked 'RESTRICTED AREA: CHRONOS PROJECT'.

Chronos? Wasn't he the Ancient Greek god of time? You are intrigued.

You're feeling bold so you decide to take a chance and knock on the door. To your surprise, it falls open. Looks like someone didn't close it properly. How's that for a piece of luck?

You enter into a mass of wires and circuit boards, higgledy-piggledy everywhere. Lights flicker deep within. It's like being inside a giant high-tech device. A tunnel leads to a doorway spilling light. You walk through into a massive room that is the opposite of the one you just came from.

It is clean, white and spacious, with curved walls reaching up to a domed ceiling. The room is a minimalist hemisphere. To one side there's a man in a lab coat behind what looks like a white lectern – there are buttons, switches and a little screen embedded into its surface. In the centre of the room is a slightly raised circular dais.

As you watch, the dais glows gently. A swirl of bright light appears in the air above it and coalesces into a small dinosaur – about knee height if you stood next to it.

You can't help but gasp.

The man turns to look at you. He's young-ish, with floppy blond hair and the thickest glasses you have ever seen – they are almost like goggles.

'Hello,' he says cheerily. 'Who are you? And why are you here?'

You explain that you're here on a school excursion and that, when you knocked, the door fell open.

'Oh,' he says, absent-mindedly. 'I must have neglected to lock it again. Oh well, security is not my problem. I'm Dr John Smith, by the way.'

That's a boring name. You ask where the dinosaur came from.

'From the Late Jurassic period,' he answers enthusiastically. 'It's an Agilisaurus. A small herbivorous ornithischian. Its name means agile lizard; did you know that?'

What you want to know is how it got here.

'Time travel, of course.' Dr Smith's answer is so matter-of-fact, as if he were talking about nothing more unusual than making a cup of tea. 'I locate appropriate specimens, bring them here from the past, extract some DNA, then send them right back.' He suddenly looks surprised. 'Oh! DNA. I should collect some.'

He takes a pen-like device from his top pocket and holds it up for you to see. 'DNA extractor. It's my job to collect as much dino DNA as I can for the chappies in the DNA department. They're growing dinosaurs and hybrids and all sorts of things over there. Very exciting stuff. But not quite as exciting as time travel.'

You agree. But isn't time travel dangerous? What if you change the past?

'Indeed it can be,' agrees Dr Smith. 'It would be very easy to disrupt history. And heaven forbid if you were to meet yourself. The Binovitch Effect!'

The what?

'The Binovitch Effect is what would happen if you went back in time and met yourself. It's only a theory, but . . . if you made physical contact with yourself, it would most likely cause a massive implosion that destroys the entire universe. A bit like the Big Bang in reverse.

'But the way I'm using time travel is perfectly safe,' he continues. 'I don't travel. I just temporarily borrow a dinosaur and then return it to the exact point in time from whence it came. No harm done.' He grins.

'Anyway,' says Dr Smith, holding up his DNA device. 'Back to business.'

As the two of you have been chatting, the Agilisaurus has been tentatively wandering around the dais, sniffing the air. Dr Smith now strides across the room and jabs it with the DNA extractor. The creature squeals alarmingly and tears off, doing laps around the room.

'No, no, no,' cries Dr Smith as he starts chasing it. 'Sit! Stay! Come back here!'

You watch them race around the room, wondering if you should do something to help.

To simply watch, go to page 190.

To help Dr Smith catch the Agilisaurus, go to page 173.

Or you could use the opportunity to check out the time travel controls. Go to page 193.

You figure that your best defence is a good offence, so you rush her. She tries to stab you with the needle, but you're able to grab her wrist. The two of you grapple, staggering around the room in a kind of demented dance. She is a lot stronger and more agile than you had anticipated.

But you manage to whirl her around, pushing her back against the fishbowl.

The bowl teeters.

'RUN!' yells the doctor, letting go of you.

But it's too late.

The spiny dino-fish spills from the bowl onto the floor. It suddenly puffs up to three times its size and promptly explodes. You and Dr Spliser are splattered in fish guts and punctured by multiple spines. Now you know what a pin cushion feels like.

'Poison!' gasps the doctor with her dying breath, collapsing to the floor.

You manage a couple of staggering steps before you too collapse and the darkness takes you.

You launch yourself at the Chook-osaurus cage, yanking at the door. The occupants go nuts, clucking enthusiastically, flapping their feathery wings and snapping their tooth-filled beaks in anticipation of release. But the door won't budge.

Behind you, Dr Spliser laughs. 'The cages are locked,' she gloats. 'You need a security pass to open them.'

And that's when you remember the pass in your pocket. You grin at her as you retrieve the pass and tap the sensor by the cage. Now, with the Chook-osauruses there to distract the doctor, you'll be able to use the pass to get out.

Except that when the cage door springs open the creatures head straight for you. Your world is suddenly a mass of flapping feathers and sharp beaks with even sharper teeth. You try to fend them off but are scratched and bitten until you curl up on the floor trying to protect your face and head.

Dr Spliser shuffles over to you and thrusts the syringe down. But one of the Chook-osuaruses gets in the way, the needle plunging into its wing. The creature shrieks and turns on its creator.

'No,' insists Dr Spliser sternly. 'Stop it, Dotty.'

But Dotty does not stop. And Beaky joins her. Together, the two Chook-osuaruses drive Spliser into a corner. Now it's her turn to cower. Battered and bleeding, you take the opportunity to escape.

The moment you open the door, however, the Chook-osuaruses are there with you. Now that they've had a taste of freedom, they want more. The two of them race down the corridor and into the main part of the Research and Education Centre, passing shocked staff along the way. You follow.

They head into the palaeontology exhibition, spreading panic and chaos.

People are screaming and running in all directions. Dinosaur skeletons and exhibits are being knocked over by the panicking people and the rampaging chook creatures.

You stand back out of the way, leaning up against the wall, and laugh. You are so relieved to have escaped that you don't care what happens to this place. So you laugh and laugh and laugh at the devastation until . . .

The Chook-osuaruses flap into the massive Brachiosaurus skeleton. As the enormous dinosaur falls forward, its skull detaches and flies through the air, striking the ceiling at the exact point where the wires are holding up a Pterosaur skeleton.

Released from its bonds, the Pterosaur swoops down across the room to smash into the wall . . . right where you are leaning.

Who's laughing now?

You reach into your pocket and pull out the security pass.

'NOOOOO!' screams Dr Spliser as you tap the pass to the sensor by the cage.

The cage springs open and Reggie stalks out. You can barely look at him. He's just so wrong!

Spliser aims the syringe like a dart and throws it at the human/raptor hybrid, but Reggie bats it out of the air with a claw. He growls at the doctor.

'I'm sorry, Reggie,' says Spliser, in her best kind and sympathetic voice. 'I really did think you'd be the first of a new species – the intelligence of a human; the reflexes and cunning of an Ozraptor. You can't blame me for trying.'

Reggie pounces.

Obviously he can blame her.

The Ozraptor drags Dr Spliser, kicking and screaming, into the dark recesses of the cage.

You hightail it out of there. As you're closing the door behind you, Dr Spliser's screams finally cease.

You run out of the restricted areas back to where all the students are. You find your teacher and try to tell him about what happened. But Mr Hendrickson doesn't believe you. He gives you extra homework for making up stories. Your friends don't believe you either.

You go back to the ferry and wait for the excursion to be over.

You never visit the Dynamic Dinosaur Discovery Complex again! But Reggie, and Dr Spliser's final screams, haunt your dreams forevermore.

You race forward to help Dr Smith. The two of you approach the Agilisaurus from opposite sides. The creature is momentarily confused, standing still as its head darts left and right, looking from you to Dr Smith. You take the opportunity to pounce. You grab the little dinosaur and manage to lift it off its feet.

'Excellent!' cries Dr Smith as he dashes to the time travel controls.

A swirl of light forms in the centre of the dais.

'Place the Agilisaurus into the time field,' instructs Dr Smith.

But at that moment the little creature bites your arm. It's not a carnivore, so its teeth are flat and blunt, but it still hurts!

How do you react?

To drop the Agilisaurus,
go to page 182.

To suck it up and bear the pain while
following Dr Smith's instructions,
go to page 179.

Your shoulders slump in resignation. There's nothing you can do for the moment. You need to follow Dr Spliser's instructions. Hopefully, you'll then find an opportunity to escape before she has a chance to genetically alter you.

You hop up onto the bed and lie down. It's rather uncomfortable. It feels hard under the sheet.

Dr Spliser lowers the lid to encase you in the plastic capsule. It clicks into place. You test out the lid by pushing at it, but it holds firm.

Spliser goes to a set of controls at the foot of the bed. As she operates them, something that looks like a satellite dish descends from the ceiling. It begins to glow with an eerie light.

'The emitter is just warming up now,' explains Dr Spliser. 'When it's ready, the radiation will bombard you with Ozraptor DNA.'

You kick at the plastic lid, but it won't budge. You're not getting out that way. Instead, you turn on your side and lift the sheet beneath you. The bed is hard plastic. But you can see the outline of a panel. You use your fingernails to try to prise it open. But no luck. The glow above you is intensifying and a deep humming fills the air.

'Almost ready,' announces Spliser.

Getting desperate, you bash at the panel with your fist. To your surprise it pops open. Inside is a mass of wiring, below which you can just make out a switch. You reach in with your hand.

'Don't touch that,' shouts Spliser, 'or you'll ruin everything!'

Well of course you're going to touch it. Especially if Spliser doesn't want you to.

To reach between the wires and flick the switch, go to page 188.

To simply grab the wires and rip them out, go to page 184.

You dash for the bench and pick up the dinosaur model, brandishing it in what you hope is a threatening manner.

'Why does it always have to be the hard way?' Dr Spliser laments.

You take aim at her head, throw the model and miss. She snorts with laughter. You make a grab for the human model and throw that as well, aiming for the syringe this time. Again, you miss. You're really not very good at this aiming/throwing thing, are you?

Dr Spliser holds up the syringe and throws it like a dart. You cower, raising your arms to protect your face. The needle stabs you right in the forearm.

Your vision blurs. The last thing you see before blacking out is Dr Spliser's kindly old face smiling at you benevolently.

When you wake up, you are in a cage. You feel different. Your clothes are in tatters. Green

reptilian scales cover your arms. Your hands have been replaced by claws. You try to shout for help but all you can manage is a hoarse whimper.

'Oh, you're awake,' says Dr Spliser, approaching the cage and looking in at you. 'I am so sorry. Slight miscalculation on my part. You'll be a full-on Ozraptor in, oh . . .' She glances at her watch. '. . . about two and half minutes.'

You glare at her. But your anger is draining away. As are all your human thoughts. Who are you? What are you? All you can think about is food. You are super hungry. And you are in the mood to hunt.

'Don't worry,' says Dr Spliser, with a smile. 'I have a large supply of live rats for you to catch.'

Your mouth salivates in anticipation. Life is going to be rather different for you from now on.

You grit your teeth and carry the Agilisaurus to the edge of the dais. It bites you a second time. You give it a triumphant glare as you chuck it into the swirling light of the time field. For a few seconds it is suspended in the light and then it disperses as the light fades.

Dr Smith congratulates you on a job well done. 'Let's celebrate,' he says, operating the time machine again. 'This machine has pinpoint accuracy, you know.'

You gaze at the new swirl of light upon the dais, wondering what sort of dinosaur is being kidnapped now.

But it's not a dinosaur that appears. It's a leafy branch. What?

Dr Smith walks over and pulls a couple of large cones from the branch, tossing you one.

'I found this in the Late Cretaceous period,' he says, picking a couple of the bright orange berries attached to the cone. 'Lots of the dinosaurs used

to eat these. And I can understand why. They are delicious.' He pops them into his mouth and chews.

You hesitantly pick one and try it. Wow! It is so sweet and juicy. Not like anything you have ever eaten before.

'So . . .' says Dr Smith as the two of you sit on the edge of the dais munching on prehistoric berries. 'It's just occurred to me that this is all supposed to be top secret. You're not supposed to know about it.'

You shrug as you pop another delicious berry into your mouth.

'As far as I can see,' he continues, 'we have two options. I could fire up the time machine again and throw you into the Jurassic period.' You whimper in response. 'Or, since you did such good work with that Agilisaurus, you could become my assistant. That way you'll be authorised to know all this stuff.'

You smile and shake his hand to seal the deal.

'Excellent,' he says, heading over to the time

travel controls. 'Let's get to work on the next DNA collection.' He tosses you the DNA extractor as the light swirls back into existence at the centre of the dais. 'As soon as the T-rex appears, you jab with that.'

T-rex?

What have you gotten yourself into?

You can't help yourself. The surprise and pain of the bite makes you drop the Agilisaurus. But rather than running away, it continues to nip at you.

You back away, trying to stay clear of it. But it lunges at you, its jaws snapping at your leg. You stumble backwards, over the edge of the dais and into the light of the time field.

Swirling pearlescence surrounds you as a deep humming fills your ears. And then in a flash, the light is gone. But so is the Agilisaurus and Dr Smith and the room . . . and the whole building.

You are surrounded by jungle vegetation – trees, vines, bushes and other undergrowth. It takes you a moment to realise that you've gone back in time.

ROAAAAAR!

Your heart jumps into your mouth as a massive reptilian head rears up over the treetops. OMG . . . it's a Giganotosaurus. Just like in the

VR game you played at the start of the day.

The creature's jaws open wide as it bellows again.

You turn and run!

Welcome to your new existence . . .

Running for your life and trying not to die in . . .

THE AGE OF DINOSAURS!

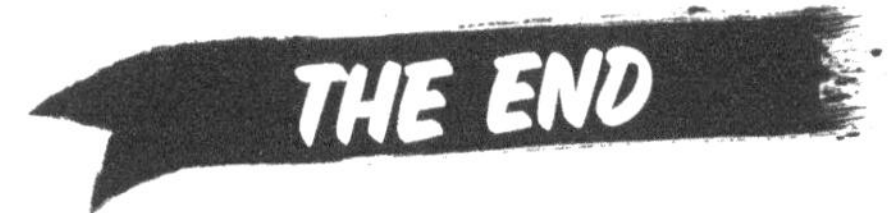

You're eager to sabotage the doctor's experiment, so you grab the wires and yank on them just as the apparatus above you starts its radiation bombardment. There is a shower of sparks and a piercing screech, as the emitter erupts in an explosion. The light of the radiation fans out like the ripples in a pond.

Dr Spliser screams as she is knocked to the ground. You close your eyes and hope that you will survive this.

As silence returns, you open your eyes. You're okay. Completely unharmed. You certainly don't feel any different. You must have destroyed the emitter before it had a chance to give you a dose of radiation.

You reach out to the lid and realise that it's come loose. Throwing it open you jump down from the bed and check on Spliser. You can't believe your eyes. She's no longer human. She's an Ozrapter in human clothing. Ripping out those wires must have caused the radiation to explode outwards rather than being focused down at you.

'Could you let me out of here?' The voice makes you jump. It's coming from the cage. You approach to see that Reggie is now a human. Wow! This is unbelievable.

You open the cage to release Reggie.

There's a muffled growling from the Spliser-raptor as she begins to stir.

'We better get out of here before she wakes up,' suggests Reggie. 'I used to be her assistant, you know.'

The two of you head out into the corridor to be met by an unexpected sight. There's another unconscious raptor in a lab coat. You look at Reggie quizzically.

'When the emitter exploded it must have sent out a blast of radiation,' he explains. 'But how far did it extend?'

You continue through the corridors, passing raptors in lab coats and security uniforms lying

on the floor. Now you start to run, eager to see the extent of the change. You race through the main part of the Research and Education Centre. The floor is littered with unconscious raptor students. You continue on out to the Animatronics Park. But it's the same out there.

How far did the radiation blast reach? The whole Complex? The whole island? The mainland? Surely not the world?

'We have a problem,' says Reggie.

You look around to see all those recently transformed Ozraptors waking up. And they're all leering at you with hungry, hungry eyes.

You'd better . . . RUN!

Why would there be a hidden switch like this? Maybe this is what will save you. You reach between the wires and flick it.

The plastic encasing you goes from clear to translucent red.

'Blast you!' yells Dr Spliser, any pretence of friendliness gone. 'You've reversed the polarity of the neutron flow. Now the room will be bombarded instead of the bed.' She frantically tries to fix the situation, hands flying across the controls, before finally slamming her fist down on them.

What's going on?

'That was my safety switch,' whines Spliser. 'To be used in the unlikely event that someone put me into the machine.'

The emitter above you whines, the glow of the radiation increasing. Spliser makes a dash for the door but is caught in the sudden burst of radiation. Safe in your plastic cocoon, you watch in horror as the doctor transforms. First, her skin turns green. Then her hands distort and elongate into claws. Her mouth and nose stretch forward into a snout. Her shoes rip apart as her feet enlarge and grow huge thorn-like claws.

You try to get out of the bed, but the cocoon is still locked in place.

The Spliser-raptor approaches you, the transformation complete, at least for the moment. She's half human, half Ozraptor. You wonder if she will regress like Reggie?

'I will make you pay for this,' she hisses in a voice that is barely recognisable as human. But her paws are too clumsy to operate the controls to release you. She rakes her claws across the controls and begins to stalk around you. Round and round she goes, in circles, her hungry eyes never leaving yours.

So this is your fate . . .

Trapped in a plastic cocoon that will most likely become your coffin.

Watching the scientist chase the Agilisaurus around the room is hilariously funny. So you decide not to interfere.

The dinosaur does another lap of the room before heading out into the outer room.

'NOOOOOOO!' screams Dr Smith. 'Get out of the wiring.'

There's a pop and fizzle, followed by sparks and a bang, as the charred remains of the Agilisaurus are spat out of the wiring. Dr Smith is heartbroken by the death, but as he examines the dinosaur corpse, a deep thrumming fills the air. A pearly luminescence swirls into existence at the centre of the dais. It pulses like a heartbeat.

Dr Smith jumps to his feet and races to the time travel controls. 'The Agilisaurus has damaged the equipment. The machine is malfunctioning and I can't switch it off.'

The swirl of light is growing. It's now taking up the whole dais.

'RUN!' yells Dr Smith. He slams the alarm switch and takes off.

Sirens blare as you race from the room and through the corridors. The Research and Education Centre is in a panic as a voice over the PA system instructs everyone to evacuate.

People are shouting and pushing and shoving, but you finally make it out of the building. As everyone is milling about outside in confusion, the Centre is consumed by the swirling light. It continues to pulse, flaring with each beat, until a final burst radiates the light in an all-encompassing flash.

You're momentarily blinded.

But as your eyesight returns to normal, you gasp in astonishment. The surroundings have changed. There are jungly plants all around. And dinosaurs. Lots and lots of dinosaurs. In the distance, there's a volcano belching smoke and steam.

You realise what must have happened. The malfunctioning time machine has flung you, the Centre and all the people back into the distant past of prehistory.

How will you survive without an organised society? Without government and police? Without your parents? Without takeaway pizza? Without VIDEO GAMES?

On the other hand . . . no more maths homework. So it's not all bad.

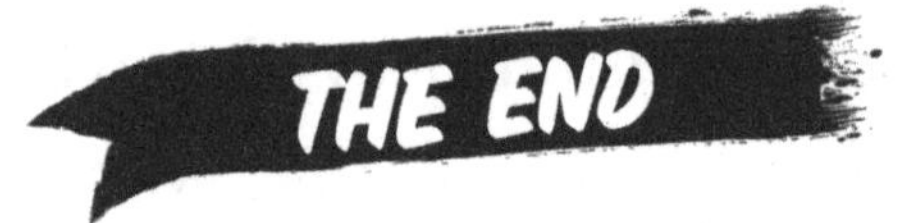

With Dr Smith busy chasing the Agilisaurus, you take the opportunity to check out the time travel controls. None of them are labelled, so the only thing that makes any sense to you is the readout showing millions of years. That must be how far back the dinosaur comes from.

The Agilisaurus suddenly races past your feet, tripping you. You steady yourself on the controls, not realising that you've changed the setting from millions of years to mere hours.

'For goodness sake, help me,' pleads Dr Smith, collapsing to the floor in exhaustion.

The Agilisaurus has come to rest in the centre of the dais. Now's your chance. You lunge at it.

But it leaps out of the way, landing on the time travel controls, its claws skittering across the buttons and switches.

You are surrounded by swirling light as a deep humming fills your ears. And then in a flash,

the light is gone. But so are the Agilisaurus and Dr Smith.

Where are they, you wonder?

You look around but can't find them. So you head back to the Welcome Lounge, thinking you might have another go at the VR game. But as you enter, you are met by an incredible sight. Your school group arriving at the Lounge.

How is that possible?

Oh no! You must have travelled back in time to the start of the day.

You'd better get back to the time machine before you accidentally meet yourself.

You whirl around and race off, clumsily knocking into . . . your past self!

Within the space of a microsecond, an incredible implosion sucks all of space and time into a singularity.

Congratulations! You have just destroyed the entire universe!

The little dinosaur is irresistible, so you agree. Princess Jazzy calls the head of the Cutie-saur™ DNA project, Dr Jane Miescher, and organises everything. Dr Miescher is a middle-aged woman with pigtails and way too much brightly coloured makeup. Her lab coat is pastel pink and she's wearing matching pink platform high-tops. She glares at you, her ridiculously long false eyelashes fluttering about like demented butterflies. She's obviously not happy about the arrangement. But Jazzy is insistent and paying another 1.5 billion dollars. So you get a special backpack containing your very own Cutie-saur™ egg.

The backpack, you are told, is specially designed to keep the egg in stasis. Once you take it out, it will hatch and the baby will imprint on the first person she sees. All the Cutie-saurs™ are female, because when they tried creating boy Cutie-saurs™, they were too smelly. The

creature has also been genetically engineered to be friendly, quiet and, for simplicity, to eat cat food.

Finally, they make you sign a non-disclosure agreement – a contract that basically says they will sue you for every cent you and your parents are worth, if you ever tell anyone where the Cutie-saur™ came from.

'Just a formality,' says Dr Miescher with a giggle and a smile – both as false as her eyelashes.

'Don't assume this means we're friends or anything,' says Princess Jazzy as you're leaving. ''Cause we're not. I mean, even if you have your own Cutie-saur™ you're still, you know, a nobody! So, like . . . *don't* call me. Ciao!'

You alternate between anxiety and excitement for the rest of the excursion, until you finally get home. You put the backpack in your room and force yourself to act normal for the whole evening, until the rest of your family goes to sleep. Then, finally, it's safe to open it.

You take the egg out and rest in on your bed,

sitting down beside it to wait. The egg cracks almost immediately and the little creature bursts out. The moment she lays eyes on you, she launches herself into your arms, hugging on to you. You decide to call her Huggie.

After a few minutes, she lets go of you and opens her mouth, making little plaintive squeaking sounds.

'Peep, peep!'

She must be hungry.

You rush to the laundry to get some cat food. But there's only one little tin left. Fluff-bucket, the family cat, has eaten everything else. Oh well, it will have to do. You rush back to your room and feed it to Huggie. Your new pet devours it in two seconds flat, then opens her mouth for more.

'Peep, peep!'

But there is no more cat food. What are you going to do?

You could sneak out of the house and go out to the local 24-7 convenience store? They probably sell cat food. Or maybe you could try to feed it something else?

To go buy cat food, go to page 206.

To raid the kitchen for other food, go to page 200.

You politely refuse.

'Fine,' says Professor Calcifeir, turning away from you with a sniff. 'I guess you're not that into palaeontology after all.'

Looks like you might have offended him. Oh well, there's nothing much you can do about it now.

Go to page 138.

Your parents would be very upset if you snuck out of the house this late at night. You decide it would be safer to stay home and get Huggie something else to eat for the time being. You can always buy her some more cat food tomorrow.

You search the kitchen for something to feed the Cutie-saur™. You grab a leftover ham and cheese sandwich from the fridge, an apple and a chocolate bar. Hopefully she'll like one of these.

Actually, she likes all of these. She devours them ravenously, almost biting your finger as you're feeding her. But then she still wants more. So you go get a box of cereal, some more fruit and another chocolate bar. Again, she devours them. But at least this time she seems to have had enough.

The following morning she's growling at you for more food. You give her another snack, then run down to the convenience store to buy some more cat food. But when you offer it to her, she

seems uninterested. Maybe she's had enough for now.

You lock her in your bedroom when you go off to school for the day.

When you return, you find your door broken open from the inside. And Huggie is gone. You search the house to find the kitchen is a disaster area. It seems like she raided the fridge and the pantry, eating almost everything. Except the cat food!

You put some cat food down in the laundry for Fluff-bucket, but she doesn't come running like she usually does. In fact, you can't find her at all. This gives you a nervous, niggly feeling down in the pit of your stomach.

Returning to your room, you see that Huggie has come home. You try to give her a cuddle but she snaps at you. You pull your hand back and leave her alone.

Switching on the television, you relax on the couch for a while. But a news bulletin catches your attention.

Princess Jazzy is dead!

The reporter says that she was found in her mansion by cleaning staff – and that she was half-eaten. As if some wild animal had bypassed all her fancy security systems and gone into her house.

Oh no! Maybe these Cutie-saurs™ aren't so cute after all? Perhaps the problem was feeding them something other than cat food? And now, maybe if you don't keep feeding her, she might eat you?

So . . . what do you do about it? Do you try to contain Huggie? But maybe this is all just coincidence. Maybe she's just a little cranky?

To try to catch her,
go to page 210.

To leave things be and hope for the best,
go to page 215.

How could you possibly refuse an offer like this? You nod eagerly.

Professor Calcifeir leads you to a small door at the far end of the exhibition. Behind the locked door is a rabbit warren of rooms filled with fossils and bones. There are people in lab coats working at tables. Some have brushes and instruments that look like the tools a dentist might use. Others are operating all sorts of sophisticated scientific equipment.

'This is where we clean and classify the artefacts that we find both here on this island and at digs all around the world,' he explains. 'We do DNA testing, carbon dating, as well as more standard things like X-rays and ultrasound scans. As well as palaeontologists, people working here include geologists, historians, archaeologists. We like to take a multidisciplinary approach.'

You notice that some of the people working back here look quite young.

'Yes,' says the professor. 'We have an intern program. Many of the assistants here are actually students.' He looks pointedly at you. 'When you're a little older, you might like to apply.'

He leads you down a corridor to an elevator.

'This will take us down to the dig,' he says as the elevator begins its journey.

The doors slide open to reveal an enormous area of earth, sectioned off into rectangular plots with metal pegs. Each section seems to be in a different stage of excavation. The area is lit by huge arc lights suspended from the concrete ceiling, which, you realise, must be the bottom of the building that houses the Research and Education Centre. At the far end are plastic sheets hanging from ceiling to floor. There's no one else down here.

'This is all pretty standard,' says Professor Calcifeir, sweeping his arm around. 'The really interesting stuff is back here.'

He leads you to the far end, pulling aside the sheets, to reveal an array of equipment that looks like it belongs in a sci-fi film. Flashing lights, monitors and screens.

'The latest, most sophisticated sonic location equipment on the planet.' He's getting really excited now. 'It was developed for military use, but we've applied it to palaeontology and archaeology. It's this equipment that led to what is probably our single most significant discovery.' He grins enthusiastically. 'Follow me.'

He leads you beyond all the equipment to a hole in the rock floor. There's a ladder leading down into darkness. You peer over the edge but can't see anything. It makes you feel a bit dizzy.

Prof Calcifeir nods at you and starts to climb down.

Do you follow?

If you want to follow the professor down, go to page 212.

But do you really want to descend into a dark pit? I mean, you don't even know what's down there. To refuse, go to page 232.

Dr Miescher was very clear in her instructions to feed only cat food to the Cutie-saur™, so you decide to sneak out of the house and head for the convenience store.

You climb out through your bedroom window, but Huggie follows. You try to put her back, but she won't let go of your arm. You end up packing her into the backpack. At least she'll be out of sight.

You race around the corner to the convenience store. It's surprising how many people are shopping at this time of night. You figure you better do this as quickly as possible. You manage to not get distracted by the display stand full of chocolates by the entrance and head straight for the cat food aisle. You fill up a shopping basket with a variety of brands and flavours. You can feel Huggie wriggling around in the backpack as you do so.

You bring out your wallet and approach the

cashier. As you hand over the money, the guy behind the counter says, 'Cool toy!'

You give him a quizzical look and he points over your shoulder. You glance back to see Huggie poking out of your backpack. A yelp escapes your lips. Suddenly, looking concerned at your response, Huggie launches herself out of the backpack and wraps her arms around your neck to give you a cuddle.

'Peep, peep!'

'Holy guacamole!' say the serving guy.

Suddenly there's a high-pitched scream. There's a biker in black leather with tattooed arms behind you, pointing at Huggie and screaming hysterically. That's kind of an extreme reaction. But his screams attract the attention of other shoppers. Soon there's a crowd of people gathering to stare and point. Some guy rushes forward to attempt a selfie, but that scares Huggie.

The Cutie-saur™ jumps up onto the counter to get away, knocking over a pyramid of soft-drink bottles. They crash to the floor and fizzy, sugary drink spurts all over the place. This further distresses Huggie, who bolts towards the entrance, knocking over the chocolates.

'You're going to have to pay for that,' says the bloke behind the counter.

But you're far too concerned about Huggie. Ignoring him, you chase after her.

'Hey!' he shouts after you. 'Come back or I'm calling the police!'

Heading outside, you see Huggie cowering in the shadows. You pick her up and start running. In the distance you hear police sirens blaring.

You round the corner into your street to be confronted by a patrol car driving in your direction. You double back and race for the park that's a couple of streets the other way.

As more sirens fill the air, you reach the park. You sprint across the playground to the trees that back on to a huge nature reserve. But the police cars have somehow tracked you there. They screech into the parking lot and the police run in your direction.

You look at Huggie, still clinging on to you. What are you going to do? Trying to keep a dinosaur secret, even a cute mini one, is not going to work. Either you need to reveal your pet, or you need to set her free. Which shall it be?

To release the Cutie-saur™ into the nature reserve, go to page 147.

To confront the police and tell them about your pet, go to page 145.

You decide you'd better lock Huggie up. Just in case!

You run back to your bedroom, but she's gone. Oh no . . . the window is open.

You look around for something to catch her with and grab the backpack she came in. It looks pretty sturdy. You can't think of anything else, so it will have to do. You also grab the leftovers from your school lunchbox as an enticement. It's half a ham and cheese sandwich. You know she likes those.

You head out into the backyard, calling out her name. You notice there's a hole in the side fence and then you can hear your neighbour calling, 'Fido! Come here, Fido! Fido, where are you?' And then he screams.

You're getting a seriously bad feeling about this.

You're about to go back inside when Huggie comes scuttling back through the hole in the fence. Has she grown? A lot? It doesn't look like she'll fit in the backpack.

She's advancing towards you. She's growling.

You toss her the half sandwich. She swallows it in one gulp and continues to advance.

Your jaw drops as she growls the word, 'Huuuuungrrrrrrrry!'

It looks like you're her dinner!

What could be down there? You have to find out.

Taking a deep breath, you follow Prof Calcifeir down the ladder into the hole. The darkness quickly swallows you up. You can't see a thing and are making your way down the ladder by feel alone.

After what seems like ages, you finally reach a dimly lit passage carved into the rock. Following the professor along the tunnel, you emerge into a gigantic cavern. Arc lights are set up and there are tools and equipment lying around. Portions of the walls have been excavated. There is a trestle table covered in bones.

'We call this the Dino Chamber.' Prof Calcifeir's eyes are shining and he looks like he's about to break into a happy dance. 'There are so many bones here from so many different species, including some we have never encountered before.' He steps over to a weird piece of equipment. It looks like a cross between a satellite dish and a cannon.

'This is our sonic excavator,' he explains. 'Again, it's adapted from military tech. What was originally designed as a weapon is now being used to release the secrets of the past. The sonic vibrations are set to the precise wavelength that will loosen soil and clay, and vibrate rock into dust . . . but leave bones unharmed.'

Your mouth is hanging open. This is some serious tech and this cavern is an amazing discovery.

The professor steps forward and flicks some switches. The machine hums into life.

'Want to see it work?' asks Prof Calcifeir.

You nod.

'How would you like to actually have a go at it?'

Is he serious? Is he going to let you dig for dinosaur bones with high-tech equipment that's probably worth millions of dollars?

But what if you stuff things up? What if you damage the equipment? What if you accidentally shatter a dinosaur bone?

To push aside your anxiety and have a go at using the sonic excavator, go to page 219.

But if you really are too nervous, go to page 222.

You decide it must be a coincidence. There's no way something so small and cute could eat an internet celebrity. But maybe you should go and buy some more food?

You race down to the convenience store and spend every cent of your pocket money on food – everything from biscuits to frozen meals. When you return you find Huggie out in the backyard. There's a hole in the side fence. What has she been up to?

And does she look bigger? A lot bigger?

She's advancing towards you. She's growling.

You empty out the shopping bags onto the lawn and she pounces. She eats it all – packaging and everything! At least it seems to satisfy her. She falls asleep there and then.

Okay, it's fairly obvious now that you need to do something. Anything! Maybe it's time to get rid of her?

Suddenly, you're struck by an idea. You race out to the shed and get the wheelbarrow. You lift Huggie up into it. Wow! Not only is she bigger – she's heavier. You wonder if she'll continue growing and how big she's likely to get.

You put a blanket over the wheelbarrow to hide her, then head out towards the local park. The kids in the playground give you odd looks as you push the wheelbarrow past them to the far end of the park. The trees here border a nature reserve. A really big nature reserve! You hope it will be big enough for Huggie.

You push the barrow as far into the undergrowth as you can and tip it over. Huggie rolls out and comes to her feet. She's awake! She's staring at you, hunger in her eyes and drool at the corner of her mouth.

Oh no, you're in for it now.

But you're saved by a rabbit. It hops out from the bushes and twitches its nose, eye darting from side to side. Huggie pounces. But the rabbit is faster. It shoots off into the reserve. And Huggie follows.

You breathe a sigh of relief and then run home, leaving the wheelbarrow behind.

A few months later there's an article in the local newspaper that catches your eye.

THE MYSTERY OF WOODLEY NATURE RESERVE

It seems that the Woodley Nature Reserve has been abandoned by nature!

Local environmental group Friends of Native Wildlife reports a mysterious decrease in the population of fauna in the reserve. They have been monitoring the wildlife in the area for the past ten years, with a steady increase in many local species. But over the past few months, that trend has been reversed, with a marked decrease in all species.

'We're completely stumped,' said group president Gladys Wattelburd. 'But we fear the introduction of some new apex predator has caused it.'

Could this also be related to the recent disappearance of two rangers in the area? The local council is determined to find out, with a team of experts planning to set up camp in the centre of the reserve.

You stop reading and close the newspaper slowly. You put the paper away and go do your maths homework. Best that you don't think about it.

You push down your anxiety and agree to have a go of the sonic excavator.

'Great!' says Prof Calcifeir as he adjusts the settings on the machine. 'Now, take hold of the handles on the side and point it to where you'd like to excavate.'

You point it at one of the rocky walls and look to the professor for approval. He nods and leans over you to flick the ON switch. 'Now, keep hold of one handle while you pull down on that red lever. Just a little bit. It controls the intensity. Then you can slowly increase it.'

Immediately, as you pull on the lever, you feel a vibration in the pit of your stomach. It's unsettling but also super exciting. You are in control! As you watch the wall, you realise that it isn't solid rock like you first thought. Earth is being shaken loose. You see there's a huge stone in the middle – the more soil that's shaken loose, the more defined the rock.

'Increase the intensity,' says Calcifeir.

You stare in awe as the rock beings to shimmer. Within the shimmering you can see the outline of bones. Not just bones, but a full skeleton. Bits of stone begin to crumble away around the bones.

'Oh, this is amazing!' The professor is bouncing on the balls of his feet with excitement. 'It's a complete specimen. And . . . if I am not mistaken, which I rarely am, it looks like a new species.'

A new species! You have discovered a previously unknown dinosaur. Wow!

'Okay, ease back on the lever,' instructs the professor. 'And switch off.'

You exhale a long breath. It seems you've been holding it in for quite some time.

'That's as far as we can go with the sonic excavator,' says Professor Calcifeir. 'From here on in we'll have to use more traditional, slow-going methods.'

You think that this has been the most exciting day of your life. It couldn't possibly get any better.

But it does!

Prof Calcifeir arranges for you to come back. For the next couple of months, you spend your weekends in the Dino Chamber, using tiny little picks and brushes to prise the bones from the rock.

The dinosaur turns out to be a new species of raptor. You find yourself becoming a celebrity, first at your school, then around the world, as television and internet news reports proclaim your discovery.

This eventually leads you to a university degree and career in palaeontology and a lifetime of digging up dinosaur bones.

How cool is that!

You are way too anxious to try out the sonic excavator. You figure it will be far safer if you leave it to Prof Calcifeir.

'Suit yourself,' he says as he adjusts the settings on the machine. He then points it at one of the rocky walls and switches it on, using a lever to slowly increase the intensity of the sound waves.

Immediately, you feel a vibration in the pit of your stomach. It's unsettling but also exciting. As you watch the wall, you realise that it isn't solid rock like you first thought. Earth is being shaken loose. You see there's a huge stone in the middle – the more soil that's shaken loose, the more defined the rock.

'Now, watch this,' says Calcifeir as he pulls the lever further down.

You stare in awe as the rock begins to shimmer. Within the shimmering you can see the outline of bones. Not just bones, but a full skeleton.

Bits of stone begin to crumble away around the bones.

'Oh, this is amazing!' The professor is bouncing on the balls of his feet with excitement. 'It's a complete specimen. And . . . if I am not mistaken, which I rarely am, it looks like a new species.'

A new species! You are here, witnessing the discovery of a previously unknown dinosaur. How cool is that?

You ask if you can take a photo and pull your phone from your pocket. But as you step forward, your foot lands awkwardly on a piece of stone. You throw your hands out to steady yourself and push the professor forward. He knocks into the machine, deflecting the focusing mechanism away from the wall and up at the ceiling, and slamming the lever all the way down.

Your ears scream with an almost unbearable vibration, as earth and rock rain down on the two of you. Within seconds, you, the professor and the machine are entombed in rubble.

You have joined the dinosaur skeleton. Encased in rock! Preserved for the future. Awaiting an archaeologist or palaeontologist to one day dig you up and unearth your bones.

Much as you would love to have a pet Cutie-saur™, you can't bring yourself to accept Princess Jazzy's offer. Creating genetically engineered pets for super-rich people like this is morally bankrupt! But what could you possibly do to stop it?

You look at Princess Jazzy. She's made her fame and fortune as an internet influencer, live streaming everything from dumping her boyfriend to having her wisdom teeth extracted. And it suddenly hits you! You'll take a leaf out of her playbook.

You fish your phone out of your pocket. Just enough battery power. You select the app, start the camera and begin live streaming.

Princess Jazzy holds up her Cutie-saur™, trying desperately to hide her face behind it. But it's no use. You tell the world about what's happening in the restricted areas of the Dynamic Dinosaur Discovery Complex – about

the DNA experiments and genetic engineering; about the creation of exclusive Cutie-saur™ pets; about how they are being sold off to mega-rich celebrities in order to fund other secret experiments.

Princess Jazzy is wailing. 'Noooo! Stop it! They'll take away my Cutie-saur™!'

You just hope that someone, anyone, is actually watching your live stream.

Your phone dies just as an alarm begins blaring. Well, I guess that means someone here was watching!

Seconds later, security guards burst into the room. They confiscate the security pass and you're dragged off to be thrown into a cage. There's a Leaellynasaura in the cage next to you. I guess this means they're cloning more than just Cutie-saurs™. The waist-height dinosaur is a pale green, mottled with yellow. It's standing on strong back limbs with short forelegs held out like little arms, and it's making chirruping sounds. You think it looks quite friendly.

But a friendly dinosaur isn't going to get you out of here.

You hope that the police saw your live stream. Or the secret service? Or emergency services? Or anyone that might be able to help? If not, you might have to find your own way to escape.

To try to find your own way out of the cage, go to page 228.

To stay put and hope someone comes to rescue you, go to page 231.

You decide that you can't wait to be rescued . . . that you will rescue yourself. If only those guards hadn't taken away the security pass.

You examine the bars on the front of the cage. They are pretty solid. Maybe you can break the sensor on the wall outside the enclosure? But you can't reach it through the bars.

There are more bars separating you from the Leaellynasaura next door, and a solid wall at the back. You take a closer look at it and see what you first think is a crack. But then you realise it's the join for a sliding door. You search your pockets for something to use. All you've got is your house key.

You jam the key into the hairline join and push. No luck. It won't budge. And when the key starts to bend, you figure you should give up. You kick the wall in frustration . . .

A small panel falls off revealing a mass of wires. Bingo!

You grab a handful of wires and pull, ripping them out. Sparks fizzle and there's an electronic buzz. The door slides back. The Leaellynasaura next door makes frightened mewling sounds.

You look into the darkness beyond the doorway to see a mass of shining eyes staring out at you. You squint, trying to see what's in there. Tiny dinosaurs! Lots and lots of really tiny dinosaurs! At first you think they're mini Cutie-saurs™. But they look a bit different. Not as round. Not as cute. Shifty narrow eyes instead of those big round ones. And then they open their mouths.

You gasp!

Teeth! A myriad of tiny, needle teeth, cramming every available space within. Gnashing hungrily.

The creatures suddenly surge through the opening, past you, and into the cage next door. They swarm over the yowling Leaellynasaura. These creatures are like a dinosaur version of piranha. Within seconds that cute Leaellynasaura is just a pile of silent bones.

And then those little creatures turn towards you, eyes staring, teeth gnashing. You back away to the far side of the cage as they surge forward.

You don't even have time to scream.

You decide to stay put and wait for help.

Five hours later, you are finally released from the cage by people in black suits. They don't say much and you are whisked away from the island by helicopter.

When you are finally returned home, you are given a reward – an unlimited education fund. Your parents will never have to pay school fees again. You're a little miffed, as you would have preferred the cash.

You wonder if you should have taken up Princess Jazzy's offer of a Cutie-saur™.

You refuse to go down.

'Seriously?' Prof Calcifeir calls up at you from the hole. 'I'm offering you the chance of a lifetime here.'

You shake your head, unable to overcome your fears.

Calcifeir sighs and starts to climb back up, obviously put out. In his annoyed rush, he misplaces a foot and slips. He's about to fall.

You reach out a hand to help him but end up toppling headfirst into the rocky abyss.

Going down that ladder might have been the safer option after all. But I guess you'll never know . . . 'cause you are so DEAD!

You make your choice.

UNAUTHORISED ENTRY

Oh no, you've been found out!

COMMENCE SECURITY PROCEDURES

You'd better get out of there.

INITIATE LOCKDOWN

You try to take the helmet off, but it appears to be stuck. You try getting out of the seat, but you're unable to move. What is happening?

RUN PROGRAM

MEMORY WIPE

XXXXXXXXXXXXXXXXXXXXXXXX

XXXXXXXXXXXXXXXXXXXXXXXX

XXXXXXXXXXXXXXXXXXXXXXXX

.

.

.

FACT & FICTION BY GEORGE IVANOFF

This book is a work of fiction. That means that I made it all up. BUT . . .

Most works of fiction will contain some facts. A little bit of reality sprinkled into your make-believe story can make it seem a little less made-up.

The Dynamic Dinosaur Discovery Centre does not exist . . . although I wish it did. I would definitely go visit! Cloning of dinosaurs and rampaging robot dinosaurs are fiction.

In *Prehistoric Peril*, there's a friendly dinosaur named Gaspar. He's a Gasparinisaura. These dinosaurs did actually exist, back in the Late Cretaceous period. The name means 'Gasparini's lizard' in honour of Zulma Nélida Brandoni de Gasparini, the Argentinian palaeontologist who discovered their first fossils. We know lots of stuff about Gasparinisaura – they were herbivores; they belonged to a group of dinosaurs called ornithopods; they averaged 1.7 metres in length and 13 kilograms in weight. But we don't know how intelligent they were or what all their behaviours were. So, I took what was known about these dinosaurs and then added a mischievous personality to create Gaspar. Wouldn't you love having a pet like Gaspar? I would!

Here's a list of the real-life dinosaurs that get a mention in this book:

Early Jurassic period, 201–174 million years ago

- Aardonyx – 'earth claw', herbivore. Cool fact: It walked on two legs but could also run on all four.
- Lesothosaurus – 'Lesotho lizard', herbivore. Cool fact: It's named after the country it was first found in, Lesotho in Southern Africa.

Middle Jurassic period, 174–164 million years ago

- Ozraptor – 'Australian abductor', carnivore. Cool fact: The first fossil was discovered by four 12-year-old schoolboys in 1967.

Late Jurassic period, 164–145 million years ago

- Agilisaurus – 'agile lizard', herbivore. Cool fact: It was one of the fastest-running dinosaurs.
- Allosaurus – 'different lizard', carnivore. Cool fact: It had little horns above its eyes.
- Apatosaurus – 'deceptive lizard', herbivore. Cool fact: It got its name because early fossils were confused with those of another dinosaur.
- Stegosaurus – 'roof lizard', herbivore. Cool fact: It had spikes on its tail for defence.

Early Cretaceous period, 145–101 million years ago

- Deinonychus – 'terrible claw', carnivore. Cool fact: It had a large talon on the second toe of each foot.
- Leaellynasaura – 'Leaellyn's lizard', herbivore. Cool fact: The husband-and-wife palaeontology team who discovered it named it after their daughter.

Late Cretaceous period, 101–66 million years ago

- Ankylosaurus – 'fused lizard', herbivore. Cool fact: It had a club on the end of its tail for defence.

- Gasparinisaura – 'Gasparini's lizard', herbivore. Cool fact: Its top teeth were diamond-shaped.
- Giganotosaurus – 'giant southern lizard', carnivore. Cool fact: It was one of the largest land meat-eaters, ever!
- Protoceratops – 'first horned face', herbivore. Cool fact: It was about the size of a sheep.
- Spinosaurus — 'spine lizard', carnivore. Cool fact: Scientists think it may have been semiaquatic.
- Triceratops – 'three-horned face', herbivore. Cool fact: It had a distinctive look with three horns on its face and a large frill around its neck.
- Tyrannosaurus rex – 'tyrant lizard king', carnivore. Cool fact: It had really big teeth that could grow up to 30 cm long.
- Velociraptor – 'quick abductor', carnivore. Cool fact: It was the size of a turkey and probably covered in feathers. Not at all like the fictional Velociraptors in the film *Jurassic Park*, which are actually based on Deinonychus.

And finally, a special mention for Dunkleosteus, a prehistoric fish from the Late Devonian period, 382 to 358 million years ago. Its name means 'Dunkle's bone' and it was named after David Dunkle, a curator at the Cleveland Museum of Natural History. Wouldn't it be cool to have a dinosaur named after you? GEORGESAURUS! What a great name!

George Ivanoff has written more than 100 books for kids and teens.

As a child, George loved reading interactive books, where he got to make decisions about the direction of the story. He has had more fun plotting and writing the You Choose books than pretty much anything else.

His books and stories have been shortlisted for numerous awards and he's won two YABBA Awards for his You Choose books.

George drinks too much coffee, eats too much chocolate and watches too much *Doctor Who*. He has one wife, two children and an uncontrollable imagination.

Check out his website: georgeivanoff.com.au.

YOU CHOOSE... THE TREASURE OF DEAD MAN'S COVE

YOU CHOOSE... MAYHEM AT MAGIC SCHOOL

YOU CHOOSE... MAZE OF DOOM

YOU CHOOSE... THE HAUNTING OF SPOOK HOUSE

YOU CHOOSE... NIGHT OF THE CREEPY CARNIVAL

YOU CHOOSE... ALIEN INVADERS FROM BEYOND THE STARS

YOU CHOOSE... SUPER SPORTS SPECTACULAR

YOU CHOOSE... TRAPPED IN THE GAMES GRID

YOU CHOOSE... EXTREME MACHINE CHALLENGE

YOU CHOOSE... IN THE REALM OF DRAGONS

YOU CHOOSE... CREEPY CRAWLY CHAOS

YOU CHOOSE... CITY OF ROBOTS

COLLECT THEM ALL!